English Papier Mâché of the Georgian and Victorian Periods

Superbly decorated tip-top table from Jennens & Bettridge with their signature on the back. The beautifully colored painting, probably an adaptation of an oil original, depicts Jupiter's rape of Europa.

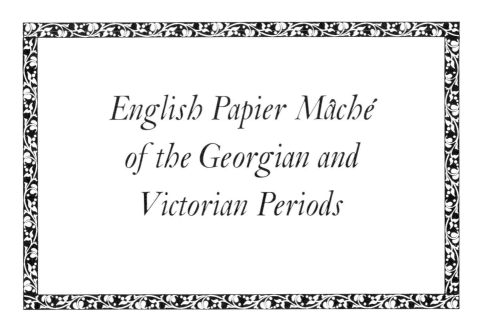

English Papier Mâché
of the Georgian and
Victorian Periods

BY

SHIRLEY SPAULDING DeVOE

WESLEYAN UNIVERSITY PRESS

Middletown, Connecticut

ISBN: 0-8195-4017-X
Library of Congress catalog card number: 76-105502
Manufactured in the United States of America
First edition

Contents

List of Illustrations

Acknowledgements

I am indebted to many people for help with this book, but I wish to thank especially Mr. Nicholas Thomas, Director of the City Museum of Bristol; Mr. Peter Klein of the City Museum and Art Gallery of Birmingham; Miss Dorothy Norris and her staff of the Birmingham Reference Library; and Mrs. Mary S. Morris of the Municipal Art Gallery of Wolverhampton. I am also most grateful to Mr. Kenneth Sproson of The Sproson Art Design Group for information about the Wolverhampton industry and for photographs of its products; to Mrs. E. W. Parker of Birmingham for information about and photographs of her father Reuben Thomas Neale; and to Mrs. A. B. Sheldon of Birmingham for permission to use various materials about the firm of Ebenezer Sheldon.

Foreword

IT gives me great pleasure to write a foreword to Mrs. DeVoe's fine book on papier mâché. Having worked for thirteen years in the Local History Department of the Birmingham City Museum, I have come to know something of the eighteenth-century and nineteenth-century products of this city-of-a-thousand-trades, and I never cease to marvel at the taste, skill, and versatility shown by its host of craftsmen, most of whom stubbornly remain anonymous, despite the research of scholars like Mrs. DeVoe. The English arts and crafts of the last two hundred years can be enjoyed and, perhaps, collected for all sorts of reasons. It is the versatility of these Georgian and Victorian craftsmen and their evident willingness to combine different skills in a product, which have always endeared them to me, won my admiration and excited my collector's instinct. A particularly fine Regency tea-caddy in the Birmingham collections stands out in my memory as an instance of this. Its bodywork, beautifully shaped and splendidly robust, is of wood covered with tortoiseshell. The central compartment holds a cut-glass mixing bowl, and the whole stands on four exquisite silver lion's-paw feet, hall-marked at the Birmingham Assay Office in 1820 by a prominent silversmith of that time. Here, combined, are the crafts of tortoiseshell-worker and woodworker, glass-maker and silversmith. In this fascinating assemblage of skills, so typical of Birmingham and the Midlands, the papier-mâché and metal japanning industries stand supreme, as this book brings out so clearly.

There is another quality of these Midlands craftsmen which emerges from the book and which makes their history so compelling. This is their adaptability. Just as we learn from Mrs. DeVoe of the varied origins of the craft, so, towards the end of the nineteenth century, the makers had to learn to apply their techniques to other products as the market for papier-mâché bric-à-brac died away. Thus, early in this century, the family concern of Sheldon, to which she refers in her book, and which has already received the benefit of her scholarship in another publication, turned easily from japanning papier mâché to enamelling mudguards for the first motorcycles and small metal containers for use in hospitals. From there, it went on to electroplating, and only Hitler's blitz on Birmingham in 1940 brought its work to an end.

From the time of Henry Clay and Baskerville to the present century, then, the craft of papier mâché evolved, flourished, and died away. It was a marvelous achievement of the ever-resourceful craftsmen of this busy quarter of England, and I find it a privilege to be associated, even so slightly, with such an excellent book on the subject. And how fitting that it should be published in the United States, whither so many of the finest products of this craft were exported. When visiting the City Art Museum of St. Louis in 1967, it came as no surprise to me to find, at the center of a display of recent gifts, a papier-mâché jewelry cabinet of great quality. And I did not need its label to tell me that it was by Jennens & Bettridge, perhaps the greatest of all firms in the business and Birmingham's pride.

NICHOLAS THOMAS

The City Museum of Bristol

English Papier Mâché of the Georgian and Victorian Periods

I

A Universal Product

There is nothing new under the sun.

ACCORDING to *The Oxford English Dictionary*, the term papier mâché, "although composed of French words, . . . appears not to be of French origin;" and indeed it has not generally been recognized in French dictionaries until recent years, when it has been defined as *papier mouillé* or moulded paper. Even if the exact etymology must probably remain uncertain, it is reasonable to assume that the term was first used by the French émigré workers in the London papier-mâché shops of the eighteenth century. At that time, and with good reason, the pulp was called in English chewed paper. The French word for to chew is *mâcher*, hence papier mâché.

This assumption is supported to a degree by John Thomas Smith in his biography *Nollekens* (1828), in which he relates a Dickensian exchange between a Mr. Twigg, a fruiterer of Covent Garden, and Mrs. Joseph Nollekens, the wife of the eighteenth-century sculptor. Mr. Twigg remarked that the house at 27 James Street in London was once a shop used by two old French women who had come to England to chew paper for the manufacturers of papier-mâché products. "Ridiculous!" Mrs. Nollekens replied, adding that "the elder Mr. Wilton . . . was the person who employed people from France to work in the papier mâché manufactory which he had established in Edward Street, Cavendish Square." None the less, Mr. Twigg insisted that his two women had also chewed paper, buying cuttings from stationers and bookbinders and preparing the paper in that way in order to keep the process secret in those days before it was mashed by machines.

"The elder Mr. Wilton" was at that time the chief English manufacturer of a substance known in the trade as fibrous slab, which was not made of paper but of plaster mixed with hay, straw, bark, nettles, and such things. During the eighteenth century he made small moulded ornaments for mirrors and other furniture and for the interiors of rooms. Prior to this time the larger ornaments had been carved out of plaster, though the small motifs for furniture were probably even then made of chewed paper. Mr. Wilton employed a large number of workers, including, no doubt, Mr. Twigg's two women.

Today when papier mâché is mentioned, it is usually the mass-produced, lacquered, and pearled article of the English Georgian and Victorian periods that comes to mind. It is, none the less, true that the moulding of pulped paper is a nearly universal method of producing inexpensively an incredible variety of useful and purely decorative objects, and that this process has been known since ancient times in the Orient. One early Chinese use of papier mâché was as a material for war helmets, which were then toughened by lacquering them. And in 1910 Ryuzo Torii discovered the remains of red lacquered pot lids in the shell mounds of Port Arthur in Manchuria's Kwantung Territory. These shards have since been attributed to the Han dynasty, *c.* A.D. 206.

There exist as well some examples of thick pasteboard made in Tibet in a remote period. The use of both pulped paper and pasteboard at this time followed on the Chinese invention of paper early in the second century A.D. The Chinese used mulberry wood and bark for making paper at first, but later used cotton and various other vegetable fibers, and eventually linen rags.

In the eighth century there was a protracted frontier war between China and Persia, during the course of which some Chinese craftsmen were captured and sent to Samarkand, then in Arab hands. From these prisoners the Arabs learned how to make paper from vegetable fibers, but by experimenting they came in time to use old fish nets, rags, mummy cloths and

Figure 1: Persian papier-mâché mirror cases decorated with lacquer and gilt, *c.* 1770–1780.

other waste materials. From Samarkand, paper-making spread to Damascus, and by 1100, as far west as Morocco. Near the end of the tenth century, paper had widely replaced papyrus, the material that gave to paper its name, and its production had extended northwards into Spain, France, and Germany. With the spread of paper-making, it was only a step toward using waste or scrap paper in pulped form for useful and decorative articles.

The Italians probably learned to make papier mâché from the Orient via the Venetian trade, and from Italy the art spread to Persia and to India. An early Persian example is a centuries-old falcon's coffin made of laminated paper. Persian craftsmen continued to produce papier mâché during the eighteenth and nineteenth centuries in the form of plates, pencil boxes, mirror cases, toys, and other small objects (*Figures 1–5*).

The Indians made similar articles on which the painted designs are often Florentine in character, designs that may have been introduced overland to Kashmir at the time of the building of the Taj Mahal in the seventeenth century. These designs are made up of small flowers and foliage, and on some examples the flowers are so thickly painted with egg tempera that they appear slightly raised (*Figure 6*).

The choicest Indian paper wares came from the studio of a man known in the trade as "Ganymede." His studio was located in the beautiful Kashmir Valley. He apparently employed many artisans both for manufacture and for decorating. The Ganymede products were signed and are considered superior to all other Indian papier-mâché goods.

There can be little doubt that the Oriental pulp products were made of waste paper just as they were later in Europe. For centuries paper-making was a slow process, and production necessarily remained small. Paper was scarce and expensive, and further use of it was sought after it had served its original purpose. It is well known that valuable manuscripts have been discovered as a result of thrifty European shopkeepers' using pages for wrapping a customer's purchases. In France quantities of small pulp boxes were made of used paper, some of it supplied by the billboard strippers, who worked all night pulling down theatre playbills. They sold any fairly clean single sheets to the grocers for three sous a pound, and those playbills that were stuck one onto the other were sold to the cardboard-

Figure 2: Persian papier-mâché mirror back decorated with lacquer and colors, (12⅜ by 19 inches).

Figure 3: Persian papier-mâché pencil boxes, the top one, decorated with a painting of a group of female figures in a landscape; the center one, with portraits of Mohtemed, the governor of Istahan, eunuchs, and various other persons of his court; the lower one, a painting of battle scenes. *Figure 4:* Persian papier-mâché casket, lacquered and painted with figures from the Armenian bible, *c.* 1700. On the lid Joseph being drawn up from the well is depicted. The pole is richly mounted in silver.

Figure 5: Indian papier-mâché pencil box.

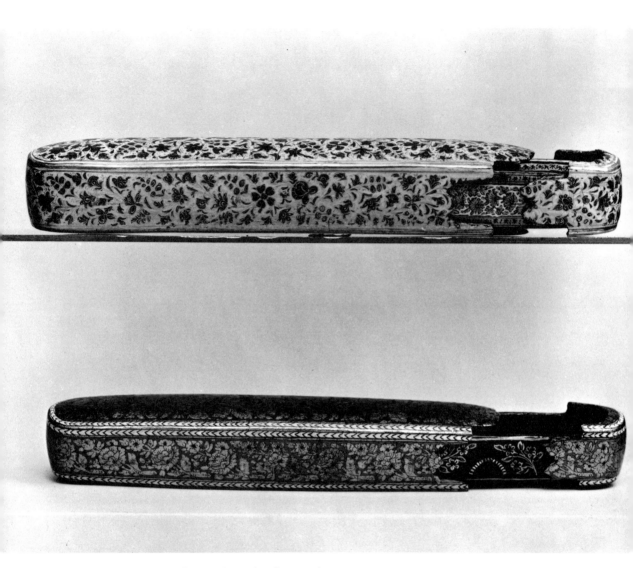

Figure 6: Indian papier-mâché pencil boxes.

maker. Ruined papers were used by the stripper for his winter fires.

The French shipped large quantities of their papier-mâché boxes to Germany, which gave to Frederick the Great (of whom it is said that he had a snuffbox in every room in every palace) the idea of establishing a factory in Berlin, which was done in 1765. Earlier, about 1747, Frederick had lured Jean Alexandre Martin, of the famous French family of *vernisseurs* to work at Sans Souci. The manufacture of snuffboxes, which had extended from Berlin into several German states, was very successfully practiced, even though at that time the products were of the rudest and simplest type.

At this time there were excellent German varnishers, but Frederick the Great was a Francophile. The earliest and best known German japanner was Gerard Dagly, who taught Martin Schmell. Both men produced fine examples of European-style lacquered ware. Schmell, after 1709, returned to his native city of Dresden where he produced lacquered furniture and bibelots of outstanding quality.

Another excellent German craftsman, who is remembered for his flat, round, papier-mâché boxes was George Sigmund Stobwasser, who was born in 1740. Having heard of the japanning trade in Ansbach, he became interested and learned the art. About 1763 Stobwasser established a factory under the auspices of the Duke of Brunswick and produced a variety of articles, among them his much prized signed snuffboxes and tobacco boxes (*Figures 7 & 8*). Other well known German pulp products were the nineteenth-century moulded toys and doll heads made of pulp and tragacanth.

The manufacture of lacquered papier mâché began in Russia about 1830, not in an attempt to emulate the Oriental products, but in imitation of similar European and English wares. The basic material was layered paper softened by heat and shaped on wooden moulds, then saturated three times with flax-seed oil. The articles were then primed with a mixture of native red clay, Holland soot, and oil. After drying they were lacquered and polished. Three coats of black lacquer were applied to the outside of each piece, and three coats of cinnabar or some other light-colored lacquer were applied to the inside. After a long period of drying the articles were then ready for the design.

Lacquering on papier mâché in Russia, according to the book *Iskusstvo Mstery* (*The Art of Mstera*) by A. V. Bakushinsky, was first done in the village Fedoskino near Moscow by peasant craftsmen who were pioneers in the painting of folk art on papier mâché. Between the years 1825 and 1830 this peasant craft grew into a large manufactory, and a particularly successful business was maintained by the Lukutin family. The peak of its production occurred under the direction of Alexander Petrovitch Lukutin. The Lukutins became the first and foremost producers of snuffboxes, cigarette cases, chests of various sorts, tea trays, and many other useful articles. Their snuffboxes became so famous that the importation of those of foreign make was sharply reduced. Products of the Lukutin family can be identified by the Russian double eagle set within an oval.

During the 1870s the Lukutin factory was still growing, although the quality of the products declined with the adoption of mass-production techniques. The business ended some twenty years afterwards; however, interest in lacquer work persisted, and in 1910 several skilled workers formerly employed by the Lukutins organized their own group called "Producers Operative Artel at Fedoskino." These workers resolved to preserve this folk art at any cost. World War I and the Russian Revolution caused the industry to decline further, and the Revolution radically changed the customs, the beliefs, and indeed the psychology of the people. For example, ikon-painters were largely without employment, and not until about 1922 did the famous painters of Mstera and Palekh find employment again, painting the lacquered papier-mâché and metal wares, then stamped "Made in the Soviet Union."

No doubt a few European and Middle-Eastern papier-mâché products found their way to England during the seventeenth and eighteenth centuries, but it was the extensive Oriental trade and the unusual interest in lacquer that brought the art to the attention of English craftsmen. In those centuries instructions for making papier mâché were published in books and magazines, and a few made reference to the Orient or to the Oriental products.

Robert Boyle (1627–1691) in his book *Uses of Natural Things* wrote that one should soak "a convenient quantity of whitish paper then mash it in hot water." J. Peele, whose information came "chiefly from the manu-

Figure 7: German tobacco box (14 by 8 by 18 centimeters) by Stobwasser.
Figure 8: German snuffbox of the nineteenth century with a colored engraving
of a rural landscape. *Figure 9:* German snuffbox of the nineteenth century.
Figure 10: Tobacco box attributed to a Russian craftsman.

Figure 11: Russian papier-mâché tray, on the back of which is stamped Lukutin, the name of the manufacturer. *Figure 12:* Lid of a papier-mâché box made in the U.S.S.R.

script of the great Mr. Boyle," wrote in 1732: "In *Japan* the people have a method of making Bowls, Plates and other Vessels from Paper and sometimes of fine Sawdust . . . [and] . . . these vessels are very light and strong when they come to be varnished and are in great esteem among us." Peele's instructions were to take slips of brown paper and "boil them in Common Water and mash it with a stick while it boils. When it has almost become a paste, take it from the water and put it in a mortar, and beat it well until it is reduced to a pulp."

In 1758 Robert Dossie, another Englishman, wrote in *The Handmaid to the Arts* that the true black lacquer ". . . has been sometimes used for varnishing of snuffboxes and all such pieces made of paper and sawdust."

But until the last quarter of the eighteenth century the production of papier mâché in England was mainly of architectural and decorative ornaments such as small gilded wall brackets and sconces and small boxes. From the beginning of the eighteenth century, the work of japanning was for the most part that of experimenters and individual craftsmen. Later an improved method of using paper panel enlarged the English japanning industry immensely.

With the arrival of English craftsmen on American shores small paper industries were established in New York City and probably in other towns along the Atlantic coast as well. According to the *New York General Advertiser*, in 1771, John Keating had the first paper factory, where he sold waste paper and made paper and pasteboard. Two years earlier Nicholas Bernard was making "paper machine" for ceilings, and in the same year a carver and gilder from London named Munshall was also making "paper ornaments for ceiling and staircases in the present mode."

George Washington was interested in acquiring papier mâché for the ceilings of two rooms at Mount Vernon and sent an order to his London factor. His wife Martha also wanted from London curtains for two windows with "papier mâché cornish to them or cornish covered with cloth."

In the mid-nineteenth century there were three or four small papier-mâché industries located in northwestern Connecticut. One was The Litchfield Manufacturing Company, which was founded in 1849 or 1850. This company occupied a group of buildings of which the largest had three stories. They were located on the banks of the Bantam River in the town of Litchfield. The directors of the company brought japanners from Wolverhampton and Oxfordshire in England to direct the work and to instruct the local women in japanning and painting. Experienced workers were paid from six to ten dollars a day, a very high wage for that day. At first the company made letter-holders, card trays, pierced hand and standing screens, and yarn-holders, all of which were formed in a simple fashion. Instead of moulding the entire article, small sections of the sides were pressed into shape and were then seamed with wire, the seams being covered over with black paper strips (*Figures 13 & 14*). In spite of this rather flimsy construction examples have survived in excellent condition. All the products of this firm lack the high gloss of the English work, and it is not unusual to find dust specks on the surfaces of some pieces.

In 1851 The Litchfield Manufacturing Company began concentrating on clock cases. They were made of a fairly thick pasteboard and were japanned black and ornamented with paint, gold, and mother of pearl. Because clock-making was a big industry in Connecticut, many companies purchased the new papier-mâché cases for their clockworks. The Litchfield company was the sole manufacturer of the papier-mâché cases, and each case bore a paper label printed on the press of *The Litchfield Republican*.

In 1854 P. T. Barnum, a stockholder in the company, persuaded the other stockholders to move the business to East Bridgeport and to merge with The Terry Clock Company, which would then be known as The Terry and Barnum Manufacturing Company. The following summer, in 1855, after the move from Litchfield had been accomplished, the company was merged with The Jerome Clock Company, though in that very year the business failed along with many Connecticut clock industries.

Another Connecticut papier-mâché shop was located at Wolcottville, now Torrington, not far from Litchfield. This was the Wadhams Manufacturing Company, which operated in an old brass-button shop. Their papier-mâché products were lap desks, stair rods, work boxes and daguerreotype cases ornamented with gold leaf, bronze powders, paint, and pearl shell in the English manner. In 1857 this company introduced a chess board with squares filled with broken pearl shell on a black japanned background, which cost five dollars. A velvet pad inside the front cover

Figure 13: Papier-mâché card tray by The Litchfield Manufacturing Company in Connecticut. *Figure 14:* The back of the card tray illustrated above, showing the paper strips covering the seams.

Figure 15: Pierced papier-mâché hand screen by The Litchfield Manufacturing Company of Connecticut.

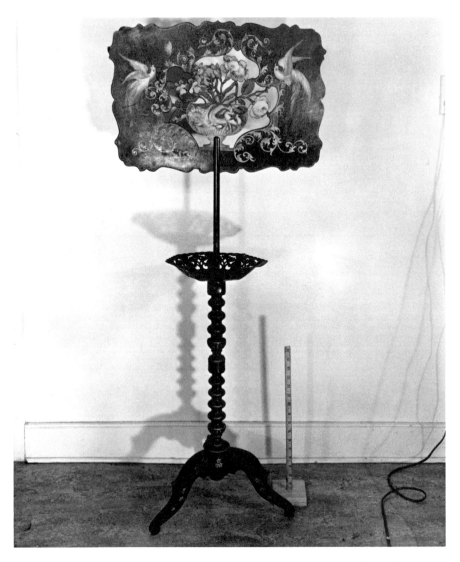

Figure 16: Papier-mâché pole screen by The Litchfield Manufacturing Company of Connecticut, *c.* 1850.

Figure 17: Clock manufactured by The Litchfield Manufacturing Company of Connecticut, with a case of papier mâché and a face of tinplate, decorated with metal leaf and color.

of their gutta-percha daguerreotype cases can be lifted to reveal the name of the firm and the fact that they were the sole proprietors of the Kinsley and Parker hinge patented on the 1st of June in 1855. In 1857 and 1858 their most popular card and daguerreotype cases were named Kossuth for the Hungarian patriot. The Wadhams Company was started about 1851 and ended in 1863.

In the Waterbury Business Directory of 1857, there is listed the W. T. Mabbett Manufacturing Company, "M'F'rs of All Kinds of Pearl Work, Card & Dagherreotype Cases, Plain and Ornamental Work Boxes, Needle Cases and Jewelry."

Daniel Cooksley, the owner and manager of the Bird Japanning Company of Boston, was born in England, in Birmingham, where he learned japanning. He employed five persons in his shop on Marshall Street about 1900. He made buttons of papier mâché and japanned them as a hobby, not selling them with his other products, but giving them away to friends (*Figure 19*).

F. R. DePlanque of 303 Race Street in Philadelphia published a catalogue in 1865, which contained drawings of papier-mâché arms and armament to be used for interior decoration in imitation of plaster ornaments.

It is interesting to note that Horace Greeley, who had married the daughter of Silas Cheney, a Litchfield cabinet-maker, was a director of the New York Crystal Palace in 1853, when P. T. Barnum was president. The Litchfield clock cases and the Wadhams Company's card and daguerreotype cases were displayed there. In 1861 Greeley became the president of The American Manufacturing Company of Greenpoint in New York, manufacturers of such practical items as milk pans, basins, ship's buckets and spittoons of plain papier mâché with no fancy decoration. A rather ambiguous explanation of the process for making the pulp for these products was that it was "based on the Japanese system perfected and improved by exponents and discoveries in this country and Austria."

All but forgotten today is that small souvenir of the late nineteenth century made of the pulp of retired banknotes and currency. On June 23, 1874 an act of Congress made it possible to have such bills destroyed by maceration. To the resulting pulp was added a solution of soda, ash, and lime, which destroyed the identity of the currency. This pulpy mixture was then moulded into busts of prominent Americans and replicas of national monuments, which were then sold to the public, a practice that ended during the first decade of this century. These little four-inch-tall souvenirs were not lacquered, but left in the grey pepper-and-salt color of the pulp (*Figure 19*).

In mentioning the various uses of papier mâché the schoolboy's carefully chewed paper projectile, better known as a spitball, must not be omitted, for it too is a form of papier mâché.

Another homely product, useful in the days of coal-burning furnaces, was made by soaking newspapers in water without a binder. When the paper was saturated, the home-owner squeezed out the water and shaped the pulp into balls about the size of a tennis ball. When thoroughly dry, these pulp balls made excellent kindling for the furnace or fireplace and were a forerunner of today's newspaper logs.

Paper pulp will always be a useful medium, as it has been for centuries, because of its strength, malleability, low cost, and, above all, its lightness. As a home craft, the making of papier mâché has never died out entirely. Such publications as *Godey's Lady's Book* of the 1850s and *Household Elegancies* of the 1860s published instructions for making and ornamenting papier mâché. At the present time there is interest in the material for masks, armor, theatrical props, and jewelry as well as for mercantile display, kindergarten work, and other individual artistic and commercial products.

Of all the uses to which pulp and pasteboard have been put, modern or ancient, none has equalled the japanned and ornamented Georgian and Victorian papier-mâché products of the English Midlands, where its manufacture reached the greatest heights in production and in quality of finish ever known. The quantity of production was especially remarkable because so much manual labor was used. It was there in the industrial towns of Birmingham and Wolverhampton that this mass-produced product was manufactured for over a century, and it is this industry and its related industries that is the subject of this book.

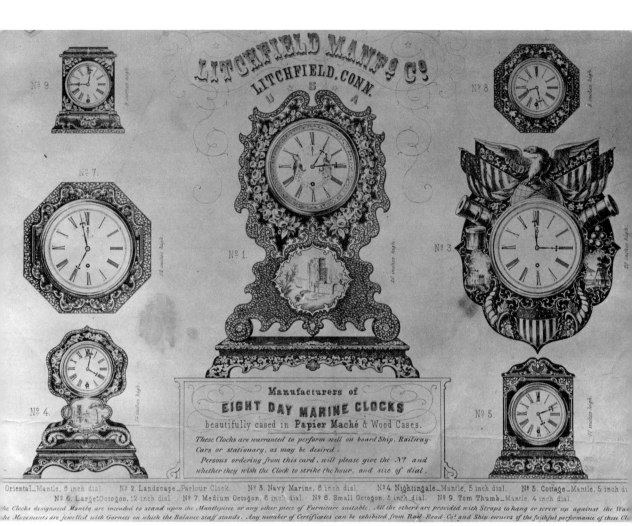

Figure 18: Page from the catalogue of The Litchfield Manufacturing Company.

Figure 19: Papier-mâché buttons made by Daniel Cooksley of The Bird Japan-ning Company of Boston.

Paper, Pulp, and Pasteboard

WITH the exception of a very coarse material for packing purposes, probably no paper was made in England until the end of the seventeenth century,when about 1690 some paper mills were established there as a result of the large immigration of French Huguenots. Until this time paper had largely been imported from France, though during the second half of the century the French religious wars had seriously interfered with the usual trade. According to John Latimer in *The Annals of Bristol in the Seventeenth Century* (1900), a certain Thomas Thomas, a bookseller of the city, together with other booksellers, successfully petitioned the Privy Council in January of 1667 to grant to them a license to operate two small vessels for the importation of paper from Normandy. From these beginnings the English paper industry developed, and the manufacture of papier mâché apparently began shortly afterwards, early in the eighteenth century, as paper products began to be used more widely and to replace carved plaster and fibrous slab.

Paper pulp usually consisted of mashed paper mixed with a binder of glue or gum arabic. Sometimes flour, sawdust, or plaster was added, depending on the purpose for which the pulp was to be used. Paper companies eventually supplied the manufacturers with the mixed pulp at four pence a pound, a convenience for those who wished to mould their own blanks. This prepared pulp was remixed by water or steam-driven machines. Pulp could also be made into slabs of pasteboard by steam-kneading the mixture, then pressing the pulp through rollers to achieve a uniform thickness, and finally drying at a low temperature. These pulp materials could be moulded by the firms that supplied japanners with such articles as inkstands, card trays, bread baskets, and many other like items.

The hand-turned moulds were made of a hard wood with a hole in the center through which the excess water and paste drained away. Some moulds had intaglio designs cut into them for obtaining the raised figures on the surface of the papier-mâché object. These intagliated moulds were called "sunk" or "hollow" and were introduced and patented by William Brindley of Twickenham. For convenience the manufacturers eventually

Figure 20: Papier-mâché bust of Abraham Lincoln, made from the moulded pulp of mashed currency.

changed from wooden to metal moulds for panels and trays, but all moulds, wooden or metal, had to be greased or oiled to permit easy removal of the dried panel or article.

Large boxes, lap desks, tea caddies, vases, and pedestals for papier-mâché tables were made by pasting the paper sheets over a solid wood or a hollow metal core. The box and the lid were made separately. Bevelled centers indicate that a mould with the shape "sunk" into the top of it was used. When the paper was dry, it was removed from the mould by slitting it on each side with a sharp tool. The two halves were then joined together and finished.

Although Henry Clay of Birmingham is given credit for inventing paper panel, it is now well known that laminated paper or pasteboard was used at a very early date in the Orient and the Near East. None the less, Clay's product was a great improvement over any earlier pasteboard and provided a much needed material for coach panels, and later a valuable substitute for a great number of articles formerly made of wood or of metal. It was this varied use, as well as its resistance to heat, that added impetus to the japanning industry and made Clay's invention of the first importance.

The Clay method, widely used after his patent expired, was to paste together some ten sheets of a soft, unsized paper, layering them in a metal mould about one quarter of an inch thick. The work was done by women and girls seated at a table. With gloved hands they cut the "making paper" into pieces of the right size and passed them to the paster, also a woman. She then covered both sides of the sheet with a paste made of glue and flour dissolved and boiled in water and placed them in the mould. Each sheet when placed had to be pressed flat with a trowellike tool to remove all air bubbles, a job requiring skill and patience.

When all the paper was pasted and the edges trimmed even with the mould, it was drenched with linseed oil to make it waterproof, then dried at a temperature of one hundred degrees Fahrenheit. The even finish of the panel was the result of smoothing it with a plane especially designed for this purpose. It had a serrated blade, similar to that of a fine saw, which was set upright in the block rather than on a slant as in a woodworking plane. The finished panel was inflexible and could be used as one would use plywood or wooden planks. It could be turned with a lathe, smoothed with a plane, cut with a chisel, or twisted into various shapes. The blank panels were stacked until ready for the carpenters. In Clay's own factory they were always placed near the workshop where the carpenters made the furniture.

After the middle of the nineteenth century a thicker panel was preferred, often nearly three eighths of an inch thick. This was no doubt necessary to withstand the pressure of the heavy die-press, a machine for the stamping out of blank forms in one operation. James Neville was a die-sinker who cut the dies for stamping out trays. Some decorators objected to his designs, considering them too showy and elaborate, and spoiling the effect of their painting. They may actually have objected to the difficulty of painting on the curves and bevelling of the edges of the trays.

Any number of paper sheets could be put together to the desired thickness, but thickening the panel, of course, required a longer drying period. For example, if a panel had as many as one hundred twenty sheets of paper, a considerable number of days was needed for thorough drying.

In 1847 Jennens & Bettridge took out a patent (#11670) for applying steam to soften and make pliable the panel, which could then be pressed or moulded into any form. With ready-made panel and a stamping press blanks could be turned out rapidly.

A ceramic papier mâché was made of pulp, resin, glue, drying oil, and sugar of lead in certain proportions all kneaded together. This mixture was extremely plastic, and it could be worked, pressed, or moulded into any required form. It was especially suitable for cornices, capitols, and other architectural ornaments for the interiors of buildings (*Figures 21 & 22*).

One pulp-producer of the time was Charles Iles, a machinist by trade, who combined colored waste silk either with a plastic pulp for making ink-stands and picture frames or with a cement mixture for ornamenting walls.

Robert Boyle wrote: "Though paper be one of the commonest bodies that we use there are very few that imagine it is fit to be employed other ways than in writing or printing or wrapping up other things or about some obvious piece of service without dreaming that frames of pictures and divers fine pieces of embossed work with curious moveables may, has

Figure 21: Papier-mâché ornaments for the interiors of rooms, as depicted in Bielefeld's catalogue of 1850. *Figure 22:* Papier-mâché ornaments for the interiors of rooms as depicted in Bielefeld's catalogue of 1850.

trial informed us, be made of it." Boyle's reference to embossed work was to the imitation of plaster ornament for interiors of rooms. These ornaments were made in hollow moulds carved of boxwood and were used to replace at much less cost the more expensive hand-carved plaster work. They could be quickly attached and were very durable.

In 1778 some Frenchman, in admiration of this English product, wrote: "The English cast in cardboard the Ceiling ornaments that we make in plaster. They are more durable, break off with difficulty, or if they do break off, the danger is of no account and the repair less expensive."

Many handsome and important buildings boasted ceilings and wall ornaments of this material. At Horace Walpole's Strawberry Hill, for example, a bedroom ceiling had star and quatrefoil compartments with roses at the intersections, all made of papier mâché. Another example was in Alscot Park in Warwickshire, where the drawing-room ceiling had "rich Gothick" paper ornaments that cost one hundred seventeen pounds and fourteen shillings in 1765, according to an article in *Country Life*. There was also a charge of seven guineas for a "sett of festoons for over a chimney in burnished Gold." When the House of Lords was rebuilt after the fire of 1834, the centerpieces and cornices of the ceiling and moulding in the walls were made of papier mâché.

The manufacture of papier-mâché ornament was of some importance in the eighteenth century, but the output was greatly increased in the nineteenth century by Jackson & Son and by Charles Frederick Bielefeld, both of London. The Jackson firm was founded in 1780 by George Jackson, who was a carver of wooden moulds for Robert Adam in 1765. This firm, still in business, made mouldings and other architectural embellishments of carton-pierre, papier mâché, and composition. They have thousands of moulds still in use, and it is possible today to have repaired any work ever done by them, from the original moulds.

Charles Bielefeld, an inventor and manufacturer, introduced paper panels that measured six feet by eight feet and were one half inch in thickness. These were moulded on a skeleton support of wood and were tough, soundproof panels said to be more durable for painting than canvas. They were also used for bulkheads and cabin partitions in some of the fine steamers of the day and in railway carriages shown at the Great Exhibition of 1851. In 1846 he received a patent for making moulds and dies used in the manufacture of all types of imitation plaster ornament, all presented in the beautifully rendered plates of his catalogue for 1850.

Perhaps Bielefeld's most interesting product was a village of ten prefabricated houses, including a nine-room villa and smaller houses with from two to six rooms (*Figure 23*). These houses had been commissioned by a man named Seymour who was planning to move to Australia and establish a village. All the houses were double-walled and roofed for free ventilation and were made of the inventor's patented waterproof fibrous material. When the village was temporarily set up on the factory grounds, heavy rains caused flooding, and these houses stood in two feet of water without drainage. The fate of this village is unknown, but there is every possibility that at least some of the houses survived for a number of years, as a church erected in Norway near Bergen in 1793 survived for thirty-seven years before it was demolished.

The Bielefeld houses were apparently an improvement over those of Charles Lewis Ducrest of Jermyn Street in London. In 1788 Ducrest patented a process for "making paper for the building of houses, shops, boats and all kinds of wheeled carriages, sedan chairs, tables, book-cases either of paper or wood and iron covered with paper." Ducrest's buildings were to be made of rooms piled up like boxes and put together with iron bolts, which, interestingly, brings to mind the contemporary housing complex called Habitat '67, which was built in Montreal by the Israeli architect Moshe Sofdie for EXPO '67.

Every paper mill had to be licensed for operation and was thereafter subject to an annual fee. The rules were clearly stated in *Instructions for the Officers who Survey Papermakers* issued in 1842. These stated that the paper manufacturers were not to use any material in pasteboard except papers on which the full duties had been charged and which had not been used for any other purpose. Evidently the English government did not permit the use of scrap or soiled paper as was common in eighteenth-century France.

An excise officer was stationed at every paper mill to see to the weighing, labelling, numbering, and reweighing. At times heavy penalties were inadvertently incurred, and all these requirements were "a burdensome

PAPIER-MACHE VILLAGE FOR AUSTRALIA.

A PAPIER-MACHE VILLAGE FOR AUSTRALIA.

BUILDING houses with cards has been a favorite pastime of many a past generation; but it was reserved for the ingenuity of the present day to construct habitations of paper. Yet of this frail material is manufactured the "village" shown in the accompanying Illustration.

Papier-mâché has long been extensively employed for the interior decorations of houses; but to Messrs. Bielefield is due the merit of applying the elegant material in external constructions; and, having been commissioned by Mr. Seymour—a gentleman about to take up his residence in Australia—to manufacture for him a certain number of portable houses, the *paper village* was executed, and temporarily set up at the works of Messrs. Bielefield, near the Staines station of the South-Western Railway. The village is composed of ten houses, including a villa, with nine rooms, 12 feet high; a store-house, 80 feet long, with four dwelling-rooms (sitting-room, two bed-rooms, and kitchen, with cooking apparatus); and houses of different sizes, of from two to six rooms. The Villa on the left of the upper Illustration has a drawing-room and dining-room, each with a bay-window; also, a hall, several bed-rooms, two closets, and kitchen. The interior decorations are so complete as to render it next to impossible to fancy yourself in any other than a brick dwelling. The mantel-pieces in the drawing and dining-rooms are of papier-mâché, have a caryatidal figure on each side, and are of bold design.

The material of the several houses is of patent waterproof, papier-mâché, and the construction is also patented. It consists of paper and rags, beautifully ground and reduced to pulp, which, when dry and pressed, become as hard as a board. There is no lath-and-plaster, yet the walls are solid, indeed more so than in half the partitions of houses built in the present day. They are also double walled, so as to allow of free ventilation all round, and in the roof. The roofs are nearly flat, being just sufficiently curved to throw off the rain. The flooring can be taken up in large square pieces, joists and all. The walls and ceilings are in like compartments, and afford every facility for either taking down or raising with despatch. One of the smaller houses has been taken down and re-erected in the space of four hours.

ROOM IN A PAPIER-MACHE VILLA.

During the late floods, these houses were nearly two feet under water, yet were not injured.

We are assured by Messrs. Bielefield, the patentees of this new material and construction, that it will make good buildings for bare park-lodges, and shooting-boxes for the Moors; as well as for additional houses, as billiard-rooms, &c.

EXTENSIVE SHOW OF PINE-APPLES.

ABOUT ten years have elapsed since Messrs. John and James Adam Co., of Pudding-lane, Lower Thames-street, sold by auction t large cargo of Pine-apples imported into England; since which they have annually held large sales of this luxuriant fruit; and t tensive trade has, doubtless, acted as great encouragement to the g and shippers, in conveying the fruit to this country in as perfect as possible. The fastest sailing fruit schooners, of about 12 burden are carefully selected for the voyage; and they are fit a very superior manner, by which means both the beauty and t dition of this fruit are well preserved.

The *Prospero, Ipswich Lass, Susan, Isabel, Black Cat* (of the two which Messrs. Adam are the owners), and a few other vessels have principally employed in this trade, and have generally performed passages in a very short space of time; some of the above-named brought cargoes in less than 24 days.

Eleuthera, a small narrow island, one of the Bahamas in the Indies, is the place from which the greater quantity of fruit is im There are annually cultivated large quantities of pines, which very beautiful appearance. When approaching ripeness, th plucked from the ground with the entire root, and are carefully on board the vessel in the same state.

Originally some little difficulty existed respecting the man showing the prices when offered for sale; but this has been overcome Messrs. Adam, who have built a new warehouse upon a very nient plan, where the Pines are exhibited to the best advantage

Our Artist has represented one of the rooms, with a fine dis the beautiful fruit.

The cargo of the *Susan* has just been sold by Messrs. Adam expect about the middle of the present month the arrival of the schooner *Scud*, with a cargo of fine pines, which will be the last this season.

Figure 23: A page from *The Illustrated London News* of the 6th of August in 1853 showing how Mr. Seymour's papier-mâché village for Australia would look.

and oppressive yoke" to the paper-makers. They complained that many of the regulations caused delays and hindrances because of the constant surveyal of their books and works by government men.

In the eighteenth century the paper used for papier mâché, or the "making" paper as it was called, was described as whited-brown or brown in color. Grey was later preferred, although a writing desk sold by Thomas Lane in the 1860s was of brown paper. The making paper was made from linen rags and was unsized so that it would readily absorb the paste and would shorten the drying process. Unsized paper was dried only once before it was pressed and packed in the legal quantities. Each sheet measured about four feet by three feet and was packed in bundles weighing either twenty-eight or fifty-six pounds. Each bundle was wrapped with a band or strip of pink paper to indicate that the tax of three pence a pound had been paid.

Glazed paper, sheathing paper, button boards, and other varieties of pasteboard were manufactured in a similar manner, but pulp pasteboard was made in thicker sheets by making up more pulp at each dip of the mould. There was always a strong temptation on the part of the "unscrupulous and less prosperous" paper-maker to avoid the duty. One evasion of the duty was accomplished by calling the narrow cardboard strips from which the buttons were punched out "Button boards." These were just wide enough to stamp out a string of buttons, which were then japanned and ornamented.

Manufacturers of integrity, like Jennens & Bettridge, used the best paper of quality for their warranted goods. There were three paper mills making this paper for the trade, one the Farnsworth Mill near Manchester. In addition to the well known manufacturers of papier-mâché products, there were in Birmingham two producers of pasteboard, W. Bott and H. Lewis.

Figure 24: An example of nineteenth-century thumb-graining.

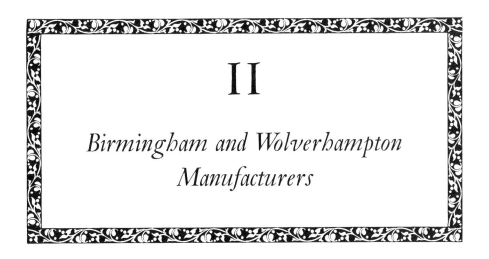

II

Birmingham and Wolverhampton Manufacturers

Tuesday, Sept. 20.—We breakfasted with Wheeler, and visited the manufacture of Papier mache—*The paper which they use is smooth whited brown; the varnish is polished with rotten stone—Wheeler gave me a tea board—We then went to Boulton's who, with great civility, led us through his shops—I could not distinctly see his enginery—Twelve dozen of buttons for three shillings—Spoons struck at once.*

—Life of Samuel Johnson, by James Boswell.

Birmingham

IN 1760, the second Lord Palmerston, father of the famous "Pam," noted that the manufacture of metal products in Birmingham had become a prodigious trade in iron and other hardware manufactures and toys in general. "Some of the most curious," he wrote, "are Mr. Taylor's who deals principally in button making. . . ." By about 1740 japanning had become a part of the metal trade in Birmingham, and it was to grow into a large and important industry by the end of the nineteenth century. The growth of the industry was aided by the introduction of papier-mâché wares, which could easily be japanned and ornamented in the same manner as the metal products.

John Taylor of Crooked Lane in Birmingham, not to be confused with the John Taylor whom Samuel Johnson knew, was well known for his gilt

35

buttons, and he later became better known for his snuffboxes, which, according to W. H. Hutton, were made of papier mâché. In the very early days of the industrial revolution Taylor was considered the largest manufacturer of japanned goods. He began as an obscure journeyman cabinet-maker, when he may have learned how to japan and to grain furniture. It was an early practice in England to enrich the appearance of furniture made of inexpensive woods by ebonizing or hand-graining it in imitation of walnut, mahogany, or tortoise shell. Thumb-graining was another form that was popular for as long as japanning was practiced. It was a similar technique and used by Taylor for his boxes. As did all japanners of that day, he tried to create a mystery about his work. He was so secretive about it that he would lock himself inside his workroom when he was finishing his boxes. He did later admit that his tortoise-shell finish was the result of imprinting his thumb over the surface of the box (*Figure 24*).

According to Edmund Fitzmaurice's biography of William Shelburne, Lord and Lady Shelburne visited Birmingham in May of 1766 in order to make a tour of the famous manufactories there of Taylor, Boulton, Baskerville, and others. At this time, no longer working in secrecy, Taylor decorated a box for Lady Shelburne while she watched him. She later wrote in her diary, quoted in Fitzmaurice's biography that they saw "the very curious manufacture of buttons and hardware" as well as John Taylor's work on "an emal'd landscape on the top of the box which he afterwards gave me as a curiosity from having seen it done." Lady Shelburne further described this work: "A stamping machine managed only by one woman impresses the picture on paper which paper is then laid upon a piece of white enamel and rubbed hard with a knife or instrument like it till it is marked upon the box [the process known as transfer, which had been first introduced by potters and later in 1759 adapted to japanned wares by Stephen Bedford]. Then there is spread over it with a brush some metallic powder which adheres to the moist part [a process of ornamentation known as free-hand bronze work] and by putting it afterwards into an oven for a few minutes the whole is completed by fixing the color."

Although Taylor is remembered today for the manufacture of buttons and boxes, he made as well toys or trinkets, as they were called, because Lady Shelburne also wrote that he manufactured much the same thing as did Boulton, whose large works were located in Soho just outside of Birmingham. It was probably at this time that Lord Shelburne became a great admirer of Boulton. He helped Boulton by introducing him to the Adam brothers, and he later supported Boulton's Assay Office scheme.

The success of the Midlands japanning industry brought workers there from the famous Pontypool Japan Works in Wales, where japanning on metal originated and where for twenty-five years it flourished under Thomas Algood. When Allgood died in 1779, his elder sons Henry and William quarreled over their respective interests in the japan works, and it is said that Henry went to Birmingham to work for John Taylor and Company. But Taylor died in 1775, four years before the death of Thomas Allgood, so there must have been an error in dates, or Henry Allgood may have worked for Taylor's successor. Other men left the Pontypool works to become involved with the Midlands industry which explains why, in the early days, "Pontipool" became a generic term for Birmingham and Wolverhampton japanned metal wares.

An important business rival of John Taylor was John Baskerville (1706–1775) (*Figure 25*), who is remembered for his fine books and type-founding. His interest in printing began about 1750, but it was the japan shop that he founded in 1748 that supported his experiments in type-founding and printing and later made him a wealthy man. The Shelburnes purchased books and japanned articles from Mrs. Baskerville, who managed the japan shop. After the death of her husband, she continued to manage both it and the printing shop.

Baskerville also produced a japanned and varnished metal moulding intended for picture frames and for furniture ornaments of all kinds. He was granted a patent in 1742 for producing the moulding by passing sheet metal through "rolls of a certain profile." The patent included the rolling, grinding, and japanning of the metal plates by a machine invented by Paul Lewis, a Baskerville employee. The iron was japanned in imitation of 'Fine glowing mahogany, a Black in no way inferior to India goods, or in Imitation of Tortoise Shell which greatly excels Nature itself in Colour and Hardness.' From the mahogany-grained iron he made knife boxes, wine cisterns, tea trays, screens, and voiders, which were long, narrow trays or baskets used for clearing away plates and knives or for holding sweetmeats.

(One interesting literary example of the use of this common article occurs in Dickens's *Great Expectations* when Mr. Jaggers, who served his guests with clean plates and utensils at each course, kept two little voiders on the floor by his chair for clearing.) Evidently there was some fault in the production of the japanning, for we are told that it flaked. It is doubtful that Baskerville himself with his interest in printing and other ventures was a japanner; he was probably, like most japan masters, an entrepreneur who hired experienced workers to japan and paint the products.

Sometime before the middle of the eighteenth century Mrs. Desmoulins, one of many women who worked in the industry, was running the moulding machine at the Baskerville works. She was the daughter of Dr. Swinfer, Samuel Johnson's godfather, and the impoverished widow of a Huguenot writing master who had taught at the Birmingham Free Grammar School. John Baskerville had earlier been a writing master too and may have met Mr. and Mrs. Desmoulins at that time. Later Mrs. Desmoulins, poor and dropsical, depended on Dr. Johnson, who gave her a home and an allowance of a half guinea a week.

John Baskerville was described by a contemporary as a handsome man, small of stature and fond of show, a trait exemplified by his love of coats trimmed with gold lace and by his coach with elaborately painted papier-mâché panels attributed to Henry Clay. Baskerville was humorous and "idle in the extreme" though mentally active. He died at the age of sixty-five, in 1775, the same year in which John Taylor died.

Taylor and Baskerville were friendly competitors and escorted important visitors each to the other's shop, and they entertained these visitors in their homes. The Shelburnes, Boswell, and many others stopped when in the vicinity of Birmingham to inspect all the famous industrial works, a practice encouraged by all the important shop-owners and continued into the nineteenth century by later firms. Jennens & Bettridge advised the public that "people of respectability may gain free admission into most of the manufactories by application to the respective proprietors." None the less, such persons were admitted only to the showrooms for viewing and purchasing. Admission to the working areas was restricted to persons who were unconnected with manufacturing and who had a special introduction. In 1849 Jenny Lind visited the Jennens & Bettridge japan shop, where

Figure 25: Portrait of John Baskerville, the printer, by Samuel Raven on a papier-mâché snuffbox.

she was presented with a cabinet by the commissioner of the Queen's Hospital of Birmingham. The cabinet was maroon with "pearl figures, Watteau style," and it was shown in an issue of *The Illustrated London News* in 1849. Still later in the century Mapplebeck and Lowe, agents for japanned goods, were careful to reach all levels of society by announcing that they respectfully informed nobility, gentry, and the public generally that visitors were welcome.

HENRY CLAY (?–1812)
CLAY & COMPANY (1770–1860)

In Baskerville's japan shop there was an apprentice named Henry Clay, whose contribution to the japanning industry was to be of the greatest importance. In 1770, after completing his apprenticeship, he left Baskerville and, in short-lived partnership with a man named Gibbon, established a papier-mâché factory. After two years, in 1772, when he was alone in the business, he received a patent (#1027) dated the 20th of November, for his heat-resisting paper panels suitable for lacquering or japanning and capable of being handled like wood and stove-dried without fear of warping. It is significant that among Baskerville's many interests was a paper mill, where he experimented in his search for a paper of good quality for his printing. Possibly Clay's proximity to this mill provided him with the opportunity to work out his idea for making the improved layered panel.

These panels were first made for the bodies of coaches and for sedan chairs, for which panels of wood had earlier been used. These warped when the japan was oven-dried. Sheet iron was available, and it withstood heat, though it was very heavy. The paper panel was therefore an important contribution to the coachmaking industry as well as to the manufacture of japanned decorative objects.

This heat resistance was the point that was emphasized in talks to visitors at the factory. In 1787 Carlos Gastone, an Italian travelling in England, wrote in his journal, which was published in 1824: "I came to Birmingham. The manufactories form all that is of interest there, among them, the manufacture of papier mâché merits peculiar attention. This article is pressed into the solidity of wood and [is] not liable to warp through temperature changes." Although it is said that Clay called his products paper ware, it will be noted that the eighteenth-century visitors to Birmingham referred to Clay's shop as a papier-mâché factory, not only Gastone, but Anne Rushout and James Boswell too.

Anne Rushout, the daughter of Lord Northwick, was another visitor to Clay's papier-mâché factory late in the eighteenth century. In her diary, in 1797, she wrote that it was "located not far from the new church" and that "they make bottle stands, boxes, tea boards, salvers &c. in great perfection." After describing how the panel was made by sticking paper together, she added "they paint the extremely well-done painting first, then lay the gold leaf on with size which dries immediately and is afterward polished." Yet another visitor to Clay's factory was Edward Clark, who wrote in 1791 in his book *A Tour of South England and Wales* that the panels were taken to a room resembling a lumber yard, which was adjacent to a very large workshop where cabinetmakers made the panels into furniture.

It is impossible to identify the earliest Clay products by the decoration, but one often mentioned as very early is a sedan chair made for Queen Charlotte. It was made with Clay's japanned panels, on which were painted adaptations of Guido Reni's *Aurora*, a painting that was warmly admired in England, where, according to Edith Wharton in *A Backward Glance*, "the simplest majority bought copies from the Roman picture dealers." In the painting the Roman goddess of dawn is represented strewing flowers before the chariot of the sun. At Strawberry Hill there was a highly varnished writing table ornamented with a blue and white Gothic pattern, which is said to have been designed by Paul Sandby (1725–1809) and a tea chest, also of Clay's ware, painted with loose feathers.

In addition to the sedan chair mentioned above, Clay made a set of console tables for the Queen, and as a result he received royal recognition, becoming japanner to King George III and the Prince of Wales. Clay's products afterwards bore the royal crown and his name stamped on the back (*Figure 26*) or "Clay Patent," and later his address "King Street., Covent Garden" (*Figure 27*). After 1812 Clay & Company used simply London with a crown.

Henry Clay, who began as a japanner's apprentice, prospered and be-

Figure 26: Back of a papier-mâché game-counter tray bearing one of the Clay signatures. *Figure 27:* Detail of the back of a tray bearing another signature of Clay.

came a rich and prominent citizen of Birmingham. He rode in an elegantly panelled coach striped alternately with chocolate and dark green and, like Baskerville's, his coach was drawn by cream-colored horses, a splendid symbol of his worldly success. In 1790 he was appointed high sheriff of Warwickshire, but in 1802 he moved to London, where he relocated his factory (*Figure 28*). Ten years later he died, but Clay & Company continued in operation until 1860.

SMALL AND SON, GUEST, CHOPPING AND BILL (1802–1816)

When Clay vacated his Birmingham factory, it was occupied by Small and Son, manufacturers of snuffboxes, trays, cabinets, panels for sedan chairs, and blanks for other japanners as well as finished goods. Little else is known about their activities in the fourteen years that they were in business. This company may have originated as Small & Hipkiss, a firm that was making paper panels in 1780. John Hipkiss was known to be a japanner in 1776, and he may have been a partner in the later firm of Hipkiss & Harrold.

JENNENS & BETTRIDGE (1816–1864)

In 1816 Aaron Jennens and T. H. Bettridge took over the old Clay shop from Small and Son. Eventually this celebrated firm progressed from making blanks to making a variety of japanned goods that surpassed those of their predecessors. Because of the excellent quality of their products and of their large production they are the best known today of the many Birmingham japanneries (*Figure 34*).

In order to keep the standards of ornamentation at a high level, this firm taught their artists drawing for which they hired a number of painters from the Birmingham School of Design.

A constant flow of Jennens & Bettridge products entered the foreign and domestic markets, a good amount going to American jobbers. In 1846 they exported to India furniture and large trays for wealthy Indians to use on the floor by their divans. In 1851 and 1852 Jennens & Bettridge had

CLAY AND CO.
beg to announce that
they continue to manu-
facture their BEST
PAPER TRAYS in the
same superior style,
and of that excellent
quality which has
hitherto secured for
their goods the most
distinguished reputa-
tion both for beauty
and durability. To
meet, however, the
demands of the times,
CLAY AND Co. have
added to their Stock
Second and Third
Class Goods, includ-
ing, among the latter,
PAPIER MACHE TRAYS,
from 17s. 6d. the set
of three.
   Every variety of
Fancy JAPANNED
PAPER GOODS,

17 & 18, KING-STREET, COVENT-GARDEN.

Figure 28: An advertisement for Clay & Company. *Figure 29:* Papier-mâché tray with a sandwich edge and bamboo handles fashioned of brass, made by Clay.

44

Figure 30: Papier-mâché tray elaborately decorated by Clay, depicting the marriage of Cupid and Psyche. *Figure 31:* Early papier-mâché tray by Clay, *c.* 1810–1820.

Figure 32: Game-counter tray by Clay, *c.* 1815–1820. *Figure 33:* Game-counter tray with bronze-work ornament, made by Clay.

their own showroom in New York City at 218 Pearl Street, a street that in the early years of the nineteenth century contained shops that catered to the American tin and japanning trade of Hartford County in Connecticut. The products that were warranted were stamped with the firm's name in small letters (*Figure 35*) or with a crown over the name and the legend "Makers to the Queen." Still another signature bore a crown, the firm's name, and Birm^h (*Figure 38*).

The loyalty of this firm and the quality of its products were brought to the attention of Queen Victoria when, on the occasion of her marriage in 1840, Jennens and Bettridge presented her with a set of trays described as decorated with such 'elegancies as plashing fountains, formal foliage and exotic birds on an apple-green ground.' Bettridge's daughter, married in that same year, received a duplicate set made by the firm. The design was then destroyed.

Another product of this firm was a beautifully painted visiting-card case, inside of which is a tiny label measuring one and one half inch by one and three quarters inch with the words in fine print: "CAUTION: Jennens and Bettridge feel it encumbent on them to appraise the public that only those goods marked Jennens and Bettridge can be relied upon as their manufacture." Under this warning, in still finer type, is the notice that "these works are open for the inspection of visitors."

Jennens & Bettridge remained in business until 1864. After that year, John, a nephew of T. H. Bettridge, endeavored to carry the business, but two years later he had to give it up. The stock was then absorbed by Mc-Callum & Hodson, a company operating since 1846, and John Bettridge became their traveller or representative. A few pieces made between 1864 and 1866, when John Bettridge was running the business, were marked "J. H. Bettridge, late Jennens and Bettridge." For a time McCallum and Hodson continued to trade under the Jennens name, a practice that makes it difficult to give accurate dates for some pieces. For example, a piano with a papier-mâché case made by Jennens and Bettridge was shown in Paris in 1867, three years after the firm ended and one year after the nephew gave up. Evidently the piano had been part of the stock absorbed by McCallum & Hodson.

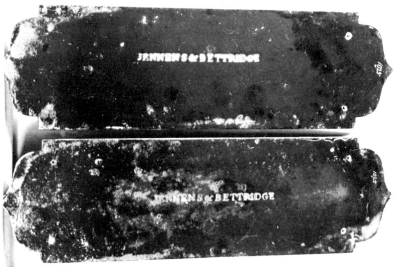

Figure 34: An illustration showing the factory of Jennens & Bettridge in Birmingham. *Figure 35:* Papier-mâché door plates showing the Jennens & Bettridge signature.

Figure 36: Nest of five papier-mâché Gothic trays.

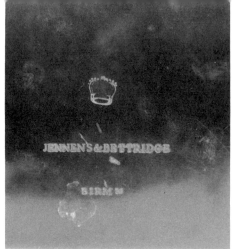

Figure 37: Signature of Jennens & Bettridge impressed on the back of a teapot stand. *Figure 38:* Signature of Jennens & Bettridge with crown, on the bottom of an inkstand. *Figure 39:* The top of the inkstand illustrated in *Figure 38. Figure 40:* Papier-mâché sewing box lined with deep rose satin and fitted with a sterling silver lock, marked V. R.

Figure 41: The interior of the sewing box illustrated in *Figure 40. Figure 42:*
An advertisement for Jennens & Bettridge from *Kelly's Post Office Directory
for 1867.*

Figure 43: An advertisement for the subsequent firm of John Bettridge about 1864. *Figure 44:* An advertisement for McCallum & Hodson from the Birmingham Directory of 1861. *Figure 45:* Papier-mâché lap desk manufactured by McCallum & Hodson, the center painting of which is attributed to Reuben Thomas Neale. The dog depicted on the life raft was Friend, who saved his master, a Mr. Phillips, from drowning and so became famous during the early part of the nineteenth century. Friend was frequently portrayed on papier-mâché and Staffordshire-china figures of this period.

MCCALLUM & HODSON (1846–1920)

James McCallum, the senior partner, had learned the trade at the Jennens firm, while Edward Hodson had been a successful businessman in another trade. It was Hodson's generosity that enabled the firm to carry on through the depressions of the 1880s and the War of 1914, when many firms had a hard time, closing or converting to other manufacture. Long after the demand for papier mâché had ceased, this firm kept on the workmen who had spent their lives in the business and were too old to learn another. One of these men was Albert Cooper, who had been in the trade all his life. When he became too old to paint well (he died at the age of ninety), he was given repairing and odd jobs to do. Another was Reuben Thomas Neale (1859–1943), their last, aging painter, who left the firm in 1920. Neale had learned to paint at McCallum and Hodson when he was sixteen, and he spent the rest of his years there decorating familiar objects such as lap desks, face fans, blotters, and boxes (*Figures 45–49*). A few of his signed pieces were displayed in Blakesley Hall, an annex of the City Museum & Art Gallery of Birmingham. Other examples of his work in possession of the family were destroyed when his home was bombed in 1941. He is the fourth figure from the left in the picture of the McCallum shop (*Figure 50*).

ALSAGER & NEVILLE (1847–1887)

John Alsager and George Neville had been trained at the Jennens firm. While in training, Neville transferred to the London branch; however, finding his wages insufficient for his needs, he broke his apprenticeship and ran off to Paris. After three years there Neville returned, and was forgiven by his old employers who benefited by his new method of flower-painting described on page 126. In 1846 Neville joined John Alsager in a partnership that was to be very successful. Neville lived in comfortable circumstances, and, when he died in 1887, he left a fair fortune. The staunch firm of McCallum and Hodson absorbed the stock of the Alsager firm in 1887.

Figure 46: Papier-mâché casket decorated by Reuben Thomas Neale in 1890.

Figure 47: The same casket from another view.

WOODWARD AND MIDGELEY (1830–1857)

Josiah Woodward was apprenticed at Small and Son sometime during the Peninsular War of 1808–1814. When of age, he worked for Ryton and Walton at Wolverhampton before joining with Charles Midgeley. They established a japan works in 1830 in an old shell warehouse, "a ruinous building that had been a depot for the pearl button trade." Woodward died in 1857, and the business ended.

Another firm in Birmingham was Halbeard and Wellings, which later became Perman and Stamp, and was taken over in 1908 by McCallum and Hodson. Souter and Worton, both partners named James, was still another. Mappleton was a well known japanner and tray-maker in Birmingham. A tray-making firm that changed from japanning papier mâché to repairing bicycles and automobile fenders in three generations was that of Ebenezer Sheldon (1827-1890), founded by the first of the name and continued by his son Ebenezer, 2nd (1859-1930), and his grandson Percy Ebenezer (1891-1954).

Wolverhampton

LIKE Birmingham, Wolverhampton has long been a manufacturing center, producing, among other metal wares, all kinds of locks, a product introduced early in the seventeenth century. Locksmithing became an important industry there, and by 1660 the city paid a hearth tax on eighty-four locksmiths' hearths. George III had Wolverhampton locks used for Buckingham Palace because of their known quality.

Wolverhampton is the oldest center of the iron trade in England, a fact responsible for the early establishment of the tinplate and japanning industries there. About 1770 Taylor and Jones founded a japanning works in the Old Hall or Turton's Hall, as it was known locally, an ancient building described more fully in the third chapter.

Jones, who had been a foreman at the Pontypool Japan Works in Wales, was lured to the Midlands by Baskerville's success in the industry.

With two businessmen named Badger and Taylor, he began making japanned wares, specializing in tea trays.

In 1775 the brothers William and Obadiah Ryton moved their business from Tinshop Yard in North Street to the Old Hall, which they had taken on a long lease. The Old Hall Works (*Figure 52*) became the most important of the Wolverhampton japanneries, rivalling the Birmingham firm of Jennens and Bettridge. As did that firm, they also trained a number of men who eventually branched out on their own and became a part of the flourishing trade in Staffordshire.

When Obadiah Ryton died in 1810, William Ryton was joined in the business by Benjamin Walton. At this time it was decided to introduce japanned papier-mâché products as a side line to their much more important production of japanned tinplate and iron products. They concentrated on papier-mâché tea trays in this new line, for which the firm became justly famous. The picture-decorated trays brought from five to ten pounds each. All firms were required to be licensed or to pay a paper tax, and on their building was the sign "William Ryton and Benjamin Walton licensed to make paper tea-trays."

In 1842, when William Ryton retired, Benjamin Walton became the sole owner of the business, but a lawsuit and business reverses during the following few years affected Walton's health, and he died in 1847. His eldest son Frederick, after a valiant effort, re-established the business, and the Old Hall Works continued to hold a leading position in the industry. It had a London warehouse at 29 Cursitor Street, near Chancery Lane. The business ended in 1874, and the Old Hall, which had been a center for japanning since 1770, was torn down in 1883.

BENJAMIN AND CHARLES MANDER (1792–1840)

In 1792 Benjamin Mander established a shop on John Street, where he produced japanned tinware and later papier-mâché trays as well. It is a rare tray that is marked with the name B. Mander & Son and can be dated between 1800 and 1820. Later articles made by Charles Mander included such black japanned household items as bread baskets and knife trays ornamented with wide and narrow gilt stripes.

Figure 48: The top of another papier-mâché box painted by Reuben Thomas Neale in 1920, decorated with mother of pearl, metal leaf, and paint. *Figure 49:* Papier-mâché hand screen decorated by Reuben Thomas Neale.

Figure 50: An old photograph of the workroom at McCallum & Hodson. Reuben Thomas Neale is the fourth figure from the left. The objects stacked in the foreground were probably face fans. The photograph was given to the author by Mr. Neale's daughter, Mrs. E. W. Parker.

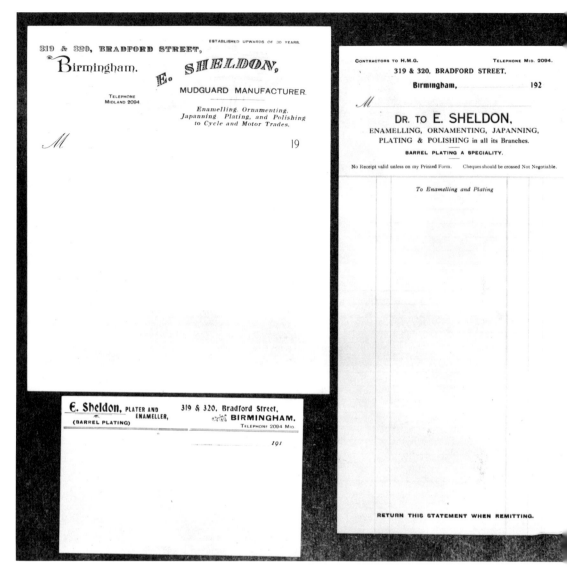

Figure 51: Stationery of the firm of Ebenezer Sheldon of Birmingham.

When Benjamin Mander died in 1819, his son Charles, a japanner and varnish-maker succeeded him. Twenty years later, Charles Mander decided to give up japanning and to concentrate on the manufacture of japan colors, paints, and varnishes. Today, as a result of that decision, the Mander varnishes and kindred products are well known in England.

HENRY LOVERIDGE AND COMPANY

When Charles Mander, a japanner, decided to concentrate on making varnish in 1840, he sold the japanning branch of his John Street Works to William Shoolbred, with the understanding that Shoolbred leave the John Street premises as soon as he could find another building. Perhaps while in temporary quarters, he and a new partner Henry Loveridge built a large and up-to-date factory in the Merridale section of Wolverhampton, which was finished in 1848 (*Figure 53*).

In a few years Shoolbred's son became a junior partner, and the firm was known as Shoolbred, Loveridge and Shoolbred. Then owing to young Shoolbred's early death and to the poor health of his father, the business was left in the able hands of Henry Loveridge. When Loveridge first became a partner with Shoolbred, he was a young man with known ability as a salesman. He travelled for the firm and was successful in obtaining orders for their japanned wares. For many years he was the chairman of the School of Design, in which position he contributed to the success of the firm and to the work of the painters by stressing the importance of good drawing and good design. This interest is reflected in the very handsome tea trays produced by the firm, which earned medals at the Great Exhibitions of 1851 and of 1862, and again at Paris in 1867.

Some Loveridge trays, usually those made rather late in the nineteenth century, can be identified by the impression of the firm's name on the back or by a printed device of a threefold ribbon on which was printed "Henry Loveridge and Company, Merridale Works," surmounted with a crown. Under this there was a double circle with "THE ROYAL FINE" printed in the frame of the circle. Precisely in the center was the monogram H.L. Still another impression found on the back of a Loveridge tray was a rather abstract monogram shown here in a drawing (*Figure 54*). As did McCal-

Figure 52: A photograph made by J. G. Findlay from an old painting of The Old Hall in Wolverhampton. The painting showed the rear view of this building, which was originally a moated Elizabethan mansion and was later used variously as a church and a japan shop until it was demolished in 1883.

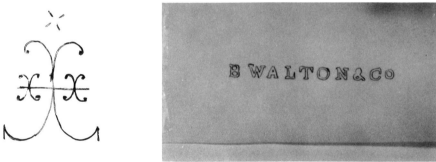

Figure 53: An advertisement for Henry Loveridge & Company. *Figure 54:* Abstract monogram used as a signature by Henry Loveridge & Company. *Figure 55:* Signature of B. Walton & Company on the back of a tray, *c.* 1842–1847.

lum and Hodson, this firm remained in business until after World War I, finally closing in 1918.

Several manufacturers of japanned metal wares adopted papier mâché when the blank-makers supplied the moulded or stamped-out objects. These Wolverhampton firms seemed to prefer the Windsor oval trays both in metal and in paper as well as the eight-inch, ten-inch, and twelve-inch round trays known as teapot stands.

These firms included Richard Perry & Son, Edward Perry (his son, who started in a small way), Jones Brothers & Company, Henry Fearncomb & Company, and Illidge & Company.

The Shops and the Workers

A JAPAN works was usually housed in an old building, often one that had been used earlier for the same purpose, as quite often one firm succeeded another. Whatever its condition was, the building had to be spacious enough to house the various departments necessary to the manufacture of japanned papier mâché. Although there may have been others, the only new factory mentioned in the histories was that of William Shoolbred and Henry Loveridge, in which the latest conveniences were introduced to improve production. One of these improvements was a new type of stove for drying japanned wares.

Over the main entrance to the factory was a sign bearing the name of the firm and the phrase "JAPAN MANUFACTORY." When a factory changed hands, the new owner would thriftily paint his name over the old, as evidenced by an old McCallum & Hodson sign exhibited in 1921, which showed the name Alsager & Neville under the weather-worn paint.

The approach to the door was paved with small cobblestones or "petrified kidneys," as they were called, a form of pavement then in general use but now a thing of the past, as is the papier-mâché trade itself. One such footpath remained in use until July of 1899, and in 1904 *The Birmingham Magazine* reported, "This was the last bit of that disagreeable style of paving in Birmingham."

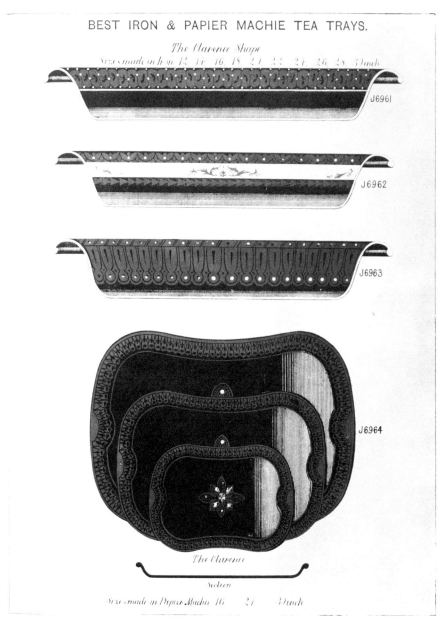

BEST IRON & PAPIER MACHIE TEA TRAYS.

The Clarence Shape

Sizes made in from 12. 14. 16. 18. 20. 22. 24. 26. 28. 30 inch

J6961

J6962

J6963

J6964

The Clarence

Section

Sizes made in Papier Machie 16. 21. 30 inch

Figures 56, 57, 58, 59: Pages from a catalogue of W. H. Jones & Bros, general japanners of Birmingham, whose company was established in 1854. These pages identify the various shapes and some patterns of trays offered for sale by the company. A notice in the catalogue states: "We shall be glad if our friends will avoid cutting out drawings from this pattern book, it will be sufficient in ordering goods to send the number of the articles required."

64

BEST IRON & PAPIER MACHIE TEA TRAYS.

The Oval Shape

Sizes made when 12. 14. 16. 18. 20. 22. 24. 26. 28. 30 inch

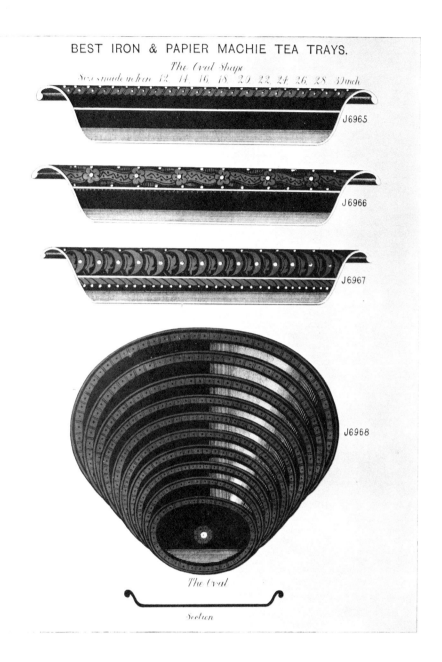

J6965

J6966

J6967

J6968

The Oval

Section

B 276
Breakfast Tray 24 x 8½ in

B 275
Round Elgin Waiters
8   10   12 inch

CII57.
Round Bright Tin Waiters
10,   12,   14 inch

B 273
Crystal Teapot Stand
8   9 inch

B 277 Registered Lorne Tray
12 14 16 18 20 22 24 26 28 30 in

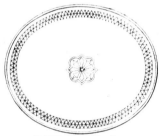

B 278 Elgin Tea Tray
12 14 16 18 20 22 24 26 28 30 in

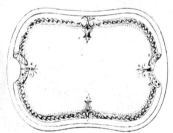

B 279 Registered Clarence Tray
12 14 16 18 20 22 24 26 28 30 in

B 280 Oval Tea Tray
12 14 16 18 20 22 24 26 28 30 in

BEST IRON & PAPIER MACHIE TEA TRAYS.

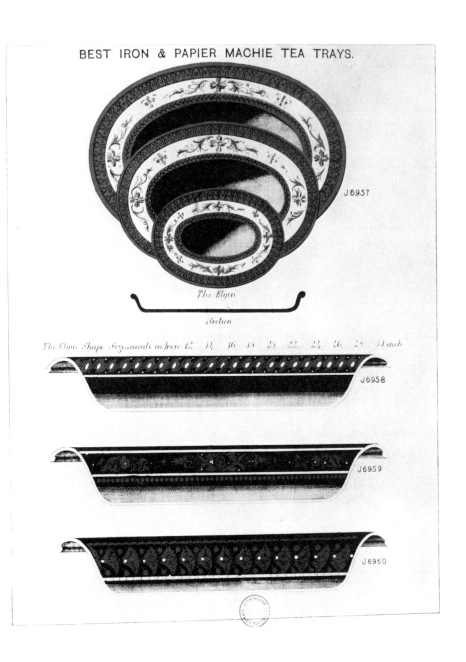

J 6957

The Elgin

Section

The Elgin Shape Sizes made in Iron 12, 14, 16, 18, 20, 22, 24, 26, 28, 30 inch

J 6958

J 6959

J 6960

Figure 60: Set of three small round blank trays from an original set of four or five, from Ebenezer Sheldon.

Fortunately two former members of the japanning industry have left descriptions of the interiors of a factory. They were W. H. Jones, who began work at the Old Hall in 1839, and J. C. Woodward, who as a boy had worked in his father's shop, Woodward & Midgeley.

The Old Hall was a moated Elizabethan mansion, which had been the seat of the Leveson-Gower family. In 1671 it had been restored by a man named Turton, but the building remained vacant for many years until it was occupied by Taylor and Jones in 1770.

This building had mullioned windows, a square tower, and a green paddock with a high wall in front. In the back there were a pleasant garden, fish ponds, and several large barns. These barns were used later, when the japanning business of Walton and Company was at its peak. In this "decayed" building, the Rytons, successors to Taylor and Jones, with their families, occupied the front rooms, and the remaining rooms were used for making tinware and japanning it. The bedrooms became storerooms, and in the large kitchen, in vats, tar and linseed oil—called "metal and grease" by the japanners—were boiled. On the floor were strewn pots, pans, and dish covers in process of being tinned. The grand oak staircase, instead of leading to the ballroom, as it once did, then led to the warehouse, where women wrapped the finished goods.

As the work in the factories was laid out in a quite similar manner, J. C. Woodward's description in 1926 of his father's factory gives us a good picture of them all. Each room, usually called a shop, was set aside for a particular step in the production, from pasting the paper to the final polishing and packing.

From the pasting shop, where the paper panel was made and moulded, the raw grey or brown forms were carried to the dipping shop, where shallow tubs held tar-varnish and linseed oil and there was a copper boiler in which the paste was mixed. Adjoining this room was the blacking shop, in which there were tins of black japan and the drying stoves. These stoves, about ten feet square with large iron doors, were the size of a small room. The heat rose to a room where the black wares were placed until ready for ornamenting. The heat in the rooms was too intense for many of the visitors to the factories. Anne Rushout, mentioned earlier, wrote that "after dinner we drove to Clay's papier mâché manufactory . . . but the rooms were so hot we could not stay to examine the progress."

In the Woodward and Midgeley shop there were attached to the large stoves in the dipping room flues by which the heat penetrated to the out-side wall, providing a warm spot against which chilled errand boys and pedestrians could lean for gratifying warmth on a cold day.

Cabinetmakers worked in the paper shop making furniture of all kinds. They used regular lathes and other woodworking tools as well as the upright plane for smoothing the panels.

The paint shop was a long room with benches arranged under the windows. On dark days, before the shops were equipped with gaslight, they were lighted by tin lamps filled with foul-smelling whale oil, which, in addition to the strong odor, filled the rooms with dense clouds of smoke. The Old Birmingham Gas Company was founded in 1817, but it was nearer the middle of the century before many shops were lighted by gas. The thick fat candles known as short eights, because eight weighed a pound, were much preferred. Whale oil or candles hardly provided suffi-cient light for the fine designs that were painted on the shiny black sur-faces of the japanned articles.

When the ornamentation was completed, the article was coated with a clear copal varnish and given several days of polishing before being sent to the packing room, where women prepared the shipments for London or Liverpool. A note among the papers of the firm of Ebenezer Sheldon (1882–1950) supplies the information that finishing a cabinet of the kind shown in *Figure 61* required five books of gold leaf, five hours of pearling, and *six days* of finishing. Many hours of rubbing and varnishing were nec-essary to achieve the brilliant, glossy finish that was the hallmark of all English papier mâché, not only on the outside, but on the inside and the back of an article as well.

A Liverpool merchant named Hanksberg purchased most of the Woodward and Midgeley products. One Wolverhampton firm advised its patrons that orders to be delivered to Liverpool must be of a size sufficient to make up a package. A discount was allowed for monthly cash payments. There were as well jobbers in Birmingham, who took the local products for the domestic and foreign markets. One was Adam William Spies (or Spier) who was listed in the directories for 1825 and 1831 as an American

Figure 61: Upright work cabinet enclosing a writing cabinet and a trinket box, manufactured by Ebenezer Sheldon. The papier-mâché covering was decorated with landscapes by Hinks and with transfer-printed borders.

merchant. His name can be found on the backs of trays in various American collections (*Figure 62*). Another was the firm of Mapplebeck and Lowe, which purchased some of the Walton products at the time of the forced sale in 1845.

The distribution of goods was very limited until the opening of the canals. Slow wagons were used to carry the products over the "old green roads," and they took weeks to arrive at Liverpool and longer to go to Bristol or London.

Once a year the japan master or his partner travelled by horseback with panniers or saddle bags filled with patterns and samples of japanned goods (*Figures 63 & 64*). For safekeeping, and in order to save space, the flat patterns were packed in shallow boxes of japanned tin. The commercial traveller rested at night at inns along the way. When the head of the firm or the traveller was ready to set forth on a selling trip, the workers gathered around him and wished him success and a safe return, knowing well that plenty of orders would mean steady employment.

Benjamin Walton, a tall and handsome man, travelled in a high dog-cart with his samples placed in the space at the back of the cart, but in his time there was great improvement in commercial transportation. There were four great canal routes that became great assets to the Midlands industries and were, according to L. W. Faulkner in his book *The City of Birmingham* (1933), "a valuable and economical form of auxiliary transport for heavy trades where urgency is not the first consideration." Then the railroads arrived, and production was rapidly increased, because shipments could more quickly reach the ports of Liverpool, London, and Bristol for export overseas.

When Frederick Walton and Company of Wolverhampton had prepared its special articles for the Great Exhibition, the townspeople were eager to see them, and Walton set up a display at the Mechanic Institute in Queen Street, which was well attended. It was with great satisfaction that the people eventually learned that Walton's products had won the highest award in their class.

A japan master was the owner or part-owner of the business; a foreman was in charge of the workers, whose requests and grievances were dealt with by him. This was a rigid rule and was sometimes a hard one for

Figure 62: Signature of A. W. Spies of New York City on the base of a piece of tinware. *Figure 63:* Traveller's sample.

Figure 64: Travellers' samples. *Figure 65:* Windsor tray decorated with metal leaf, pearl, and paint, signed Jennens & Bettridge.

a man with a real grievance, especially if there were a conflict of personality between the foreman and himself. A case in point is the one of Frederick Newman, a painter employed at Walton and Company. Newman had become over-enthusiastic about peacocks, placing them "in environs suitable and unsuitable" in his tray designs. The foreman, who disliked Newman, also disliked his peacocks, and a flare-up ensued when the foreman erased the peacocks from some trays. The result was a court action, which Newman won owing to the foreman's having erased the evidence. None the less, Newman was discharged, though he soon found work at Loveridge and Company.

In addition to the master and the foreman there were men and boys and girls and women employed in the various subdivisions of the industry. Many young people followed their parents in the occupation. These workers were pasters, moulders, carpenters, blackers, painters, pearlers, borderers, filleters, polishers, and packers, and many became experienced enough to do work in more than one area.

In the early days of the industry the boys and girls were often very young, and they had no opportunity to go to school. At that time there was no outside interest to bring pressure to bear on the parents to have their children learn even to read and reckon. But the earnings of the children, however meager, were necessary to the subsistence of the family, and since trade was flourishing the future did not seem altogether bleak. Wages were extremely low and remained low always. A boy's pay was two shillings and six pence a week; after seven years it rose to seven shillings and six pence. Overtime started at one pence and rose to four pence. Painters earned from thirty to fifty shillings a week, and even in the 1890s a painter still earned only thirty shillings a week. One painter working for John Taylor in the 1760s earned three shillings and ten pence a week by painting the snuffboxes at a farthing each. In New York City in 1863, women japanners earned from three to four dollars a week, and ornamental painters earned from five to ten dollars a week, according to *The Employment of Women*, a book written by Virginia Penny in that year.

Boys were trained in the branch of the business that suited their capabilities, and at other times they were required to run errands. Early in the nineteenth century, during the Peninsular War, the news of the progress

Figure 66: A thirty-inch King Gothic tray with exceptionally fine ornamentation, using all the known techniques of decoration—gold leaf, free-hand bronze, painting on black japan, and floating color. *Figure 67:* Another Windsor tray, oval in shape and with exceptionally fine ornament, including freehand bronze work, gold leaf and painting, signed "Mechi."

76

of the brave British soldiers and sailors was naturally of keen interest to the people at home, and in order to give the workers news of developments, a boy was daily sent to await the arrival of the Royal Mail, which would bring the latest word of Wellington's progress. Even though the apprentice system was disappearing after 1850, boys were still taught a trade when in their teens.

Occasionally the tedium of working hours was relieved by some form of good-natured banter between departments, banter that sometimes took the form of satirical verse placed on the bulletin board. Some of the artists were gifted caricaturists and amused their coworkers by drawing likenesses of them or of someone else whom they all knew. In all, there were many lighter moments provided in a long and busy day at a time when working conditions were anything but ideal, by today's standards at least.

The working hours were very long. They began at seven o'clock in the morning and ended at eight o'clock in the evening, six days a week, summer and winter. By the middle of the nineteenth century there was a little improvement: the working day began at eight o'clock and ended at seven o'clock on week days and at six o'clock on Saturdays. A bell summoned the employees to work and later announced quitting time. The painters at Woodward's dubbed the quitting bell "salvation."

These workers were not members of the guild or of a union, but they knew one another and shared the same habits and pleasures. Their evenings were spent at public houses like The Red Lion, The Wool Pack, and The Snow Hill, where over a pint such topics as the merits of a champion of the prize ring, racing, politics, or various grievances caused by the foreman were thoroughly discussed and argued. The snuffbox was passed around and around, and clay pipes were smoked. In those days they seldom went home before midnight.

Papier-Mâché Manufacturers and Dealers of Birmingham and Wolverhampton from 1770.

S. Adderley & Sons
Alsager & Neville
Joseph Arrowsmith
John Bakewell
John Baskerville
Stephen Bedford
Bill & Company
Mr. Brindley
Francis Byrne
T. Chatterley
Clay & Gibbons, later Henry Clay &
    Company*
G. C. Davies*
John Dean & Son
Charles Docker
Edmunds, Gill, Millwards &
    Westwood
James Fellows & Sons
William Fletcher
Footherope, Shewell & Shenston
R. Gardner
Grice & Dickinson
Halbeard & Stamps, later Halbeard &
    Wellings*
Harker & Shakspeare
A & A Hewson
John Hipkiss
Hipkiss & Harrold
Richard Hipkiss
Thomas Illidge
M. L. Jacob
Jennens & Bettridge*
Thomas Lane*

William Leeson & Son
Littleholes & Green
McCallum & Hodson*
Benjamin Mander, later
    Charles Mander
James Matlow
Moreton & Taunton
G. Morley
S. P. Nock
William Parkes
James Pedley
Thomas Phillips
C. P. Pitt
John Price
Ryton & Sons, later Ryton & Walton
James Salt
C. Sanders
Joseph Sankey
John Sankey
John Savage
J. Sheldon
Ebenezer Sheldon
Ebenezer Sheldon, Jr.
Percy Ebenezer Sheldon
Shoolbred, Loveridge & Shoolbred,*
    later Loveridge & Shoolbred,
    then H. Loveridge & Company
Thomas Smalls & Son
Small & Son, Guest, Chopping and Bill
Joseph Smith
Solomon & Jacob
I. Sutcliffe*
John Taylor

*Firms marked with an asterisk exhibited at the Great Exhibition of 1851 at the
  Crystal Palace in London.

R. Turley
G. Vale & Son
Hezekiah Walker
Benjamin Walton, later Frederick
    Walton & Company*
Watson & Company

John Webb
Thomas Wharton
John P. Whitehead
J. Whitehouse
George Welles
Robert Winn

Figure 68: Papier-mâché Gothic tray manufactured by Clay.

III

Ornamentation

Japan and Varnish

I enter upon a difficult Point to give you sufficient instructions in the Art of Japanning *since so many Niceties are in it; however, what I send is tho' short, to the purpose.*—"Your humble servant and friend, J. H.," from Gentlemen's Magazine, February, 1736.

THE English imitation of lacquer, called japan, was named for the country, because the true Japanese product was considered superior to other Eastern lacquers, and the English artisans hoped to equal it. That they were successful to a degree we learn from *A Collection of Husbandry and Trade* (1694), which states: "Japan is brought to that perfection it not only outdoes all that is made in India but . . . the Japan lacquer itself; and there is hope of imitating its best draught and figures."

Oriental lacquer was introduced to Europe and to England by the East India Companies of Portugal, Holland, and England. On the 20th of April in 1661 Samuel Pepys saw in a closet at the Duke of York's "two very fine chests covered with gold and Indian varnish, given by the East Indy Company of Holland." The terms India and Indian became attached to all Eastern lacquers and other like products when the Dutch, who proclaimed themselves "lords of the Seven Seas," denied traffic to China and Japan, to all ships but their own. This embargo forced the English for a time to load their cargoes on the Indian coast, where they had been deposited by Oriental vessels, a fact that explains why the incised Chinese lacquer screens are called Coromandel (*Figure 69*).

The Oriental or "Indian" style gained such popularity with the court and the great families that imitating lacquer became the immediate concern of cabinetmakers and other artisans; however, an easily obtained native substitute for the true Oriental lacquer was required.

The basis for true Oriental lacquer was the sap of a tree indigenous to the Orient, the *Rhus vernicifera*. The use of this lacquer, or rhuslack, was not practical in the West, because it involved a very complicated, delicate technique successfully achieved only after years of experience. Too, rhuslack did not respond to dry heat, but hardened in about four hours in a damp atmosphere at a temperature of about seventy degrees Fahrenheit. There was as well the consideration that the poisonous virulence of this member of the sumac family caused an extreme dermatitis in humans. So sensitive are some people to this substance that they cannot even remain in a room full of finished lacquer wares. These two problems encouraged the development of lacquer or varnish in the West. Varnish, of course, was not a new substance, as it was known from the time of the Egyptians. Later, in the Byzantine period, it was made from a solution of rosin and linseed oil, and it was widely used for gilding and protecting pictures. By the fourteenth century varnishers were listed with carpenters and gilders in the membership of the Painters Guild of Venice. At about that time a kind of rosin called Greek pitch was introduced to the West through Venice and was used under various names in various ways. In the seventeenth century scientists in Europe and in England were searching for a formula for a good varnish, to be used not only as a substitute for lacquer but as a standard hard, glossy, and weather-proof coating for sedan chairs and coaches.

The Martin Brothers of Paris, coach-painters and varnishers, had ample opportunities for testing varnishes in their daily occupation. They finally achieved the famous *Vernis Martin*, which in later years became a generic term for many painted and varnished articles, which were seldom the equal of the work of the brothers Martin. Their varnish was not, however, their own invention, but was developed by improving the mixtures

Figure 69: Panel from the border of a tubular lacquered screen. This beautiful screen is Chinese, made during the K'ang-Hsi period, between 1662 and 1722, for Fong Long, the Kon of Fatshan, probably about 1690. It beautifully exemplifies the usual motifs of a so-called Coromandel screen.

in general use at the time, among which the principal was that of Christian Huygens (1629–1695), the Dutch inventor of the first successful varnish of the period.

In England, the great Robert Boyle described his first attempt at imitating Chinese and Japanese lacquer with shellac: "I am credibly informed that the art of making the like varnished ware is now begun to be a trade at Paris and doubt not but it will be so in London too." This information proved to be true, for in 1736 Robert Price was employed in the Royal household to embellish furniture with China varnish, and there were others in London, in the Midlands, and in Wales who were then working at the trade.

In 1759 The Society for the Encouragement of the Arts, Manufactures, and Commerce offered premiums for the development of a number of things, one for the best varnish. In 1763 Stephen Bedford of Birmingham was given an award by The Society for his varnish formula that, when tested, was considered "almost equal to the contemporary copal varnish of the famous Martin brothers." By 1770 Bedford was "more renowned than Taylor or Baskerville though thenceforward his main output was of lacquered papier mâché goods." He died in 1781.

The first instructions for the making of varnish to be used to imitate lacquer appeared in G. Stalker and J. Parker's *A Treatise of Japanning and Varnishing* in 1688. The following year Sir Edmund Verney wrote to his daughter, who was then away at school, a letter quoted in *Connoisseur* (July–December, 1929): "I find that you have a desire to learn to Jappan as you call it and approve. To learn this art costs a guinea entrance and some 40 shillings more to work on." After the publication of Stalker and Parker's *A Treatise* other books containing instructions for japanning were issued: *Polygraphice* by William Salmon, the first of eight editions appearing in 1701; *The Handmaid to the Arts* by Robert Dossie in 1758; and *The Ladies Amusement* by Robert Sayer in 1760. In 1732 J. Peele published a small book entitled *A New and Curious Method of Japanning*, which he dedicated to Lady Walpole, Horace Walpole's mother, no doubt for a consideration, then the practice. It is quite possible that she had received instruction from Peele, because it is known that she was interested in and practiced a variety of the so-called genteel arts of her day, including

Figure 70: Decorated tray showing Indian flowers and other motifs adapted from Oriental lacquer work.

Figure 71: A lacquered table decorated with Indian work, eighteenth-century.
Notice the careful striping.

japanning. It is said that her son kept an example of her japan work at Strawberry Hill.

Peele's tribute to Lady Walpole was as follows: "As your ladyship is distinguished for your excellent Performance in Painting, Japanning and many other Curious Arts, I beg leave to lay before you a few experienced Receipts which have never yet appeared in the World. Many of them I have been at great Pains and Expense to procure and for the rest I am obliged to some mss of the Great Mr. Boyle. Tis by the influence of his name that I venture to address this little treatise to your Ladyship which I persuade myself will not be unacceptable to you as I am sure the Experiments therein contained will fully answer their several intentions."

Japanning became a popular art among the ladies of the eighteenth century, and *The Burlington Magazine* and *The Gentlemen's Magazine* published articles describing the newest methods. Advertisements were placed in eighteenth-century English and American newspapers by teachers of japanning and other genteel arts, all of which were taught at girls' schools. Ten-year-old Nellie Custis, who was to attend Mrs. Graham's school in Maiden Lane in New York City as a day pupil, was to learn such extra accomplishments as drawing, japanning, filigreeing, and French.

Although colored grounds were sometimes used, black was the base coat of the majority of papier-mâché japanned wares, and a black tar varnish made of a mixture of amber, linseed oil, rosin, and asphaltum thinned with turpentine was used.

Asphalt or asphaltum was a slow-drying element made from the residue of petroleum or coal tar, hence the term tar varnish. It was also a natural product of the Dead Sea, and in early times it was known as Jewish pitch. In biblical days this bituminous substance was used to waterproof the hulls of sea-going craft. In *Genesis* (VI:4) it is recorded that, when God commanded Noah to build an ark of gopher wood, he was also told: "Rooms shalt thou make in the ark and shall pitch it within and without."

Asphaltum was known and used in eighteenth-century Europe as a coating for the bodies of vehicles. In *The Treatise on Sedan Chairs* (1737) H. X. Schramm wrote: "The Chinese like to paint their Sedan chairs with a kind of Jewish glue so that they shone like mirrors." Undoubtedly, what he thought was "a kind of Jewish glue," was really the natural lacquer used in the Orient before the Christian era and not then known to the Western world.

Oil varnish was the most important for general use. It consisted of linseed oil, rosins, and spirits of turpentine. A spirit varnish was made by dissolving shellac in alcohol. This solution dried rapidly to a hard, brittle surface. Lamp black was added to clear varnish to obtain black, and eventually any color desired could be obtained by combining the so-called "mixing varnishes," manufactured specifically for this purpose, with various coloring agents.

In the early days many japanners made their own varnish, a dangerous job, for the materials were all highly inflammable. It was safer to cook the varnish outdoors, because the burning substance was difficult to extinguish. The person attending the varnish was advised to wear dampened leather gloves or to keep a wet blanket handy. (One wonders if this were the origin of the term.) A sand bath was another safety measure. The varnish vessel was placed in another vessel, which was filled with sand and then placed on the fire. This procedure not only prevented the varnish from becoming over-heated, but also kept the fluid warm so that it flowed more readily from the brush. In time all painted and varnished pieces were called japan, even into the twentieth century. Not only was this true of painted and decorated furniture and metal wares, but also in the early bicycle and automobile industries. There was little difference in the coating of metal with japan or enamel, either a mudguard, a tray, or the body of a vehicle. The early bicycle and motor industries needed japanners and filletters, thus permitting William Sheldon and other japanners to move from papier mâché to the new industry.

In all its uses japan varnish provided a substitute for better materials. Just as gold leaf was used in imitations of ormolu on japanned furniture, and as precisely painted designs imitated wood inlays, so japan, in the form of wood-graining and ebonizing on native woods and papier mâché, provided attractive finishes at less cost. But it was the use of japan varnish as a substitute for Oriental lacquer that was the beginning of the great English japanning and ornamenting industry from which many related industries sprang.

88

Figure 72: Papier-mâché parlour-maid's tray. *Figure 73:* King Gothic tray by H. Loveridge & Company.

Figure 74: A convex King Gothic tray signed Clay. *Figure 75:* Sandwich-edge tray with finely executed bronze background with cloud effects. The decoration on this tray is a beautiful example of the best English workmanship during the 1840s.

Gold and Other Metals

Do not hold everything as gold that shines like gold.
—Alanus de Insulis, 1294.

GOLD, the most precious and the most ductile of all metals, was used in leaf form in ancient countries to decorate a great variety of things. In sixteenth-century Venice it was used to cover iron, marble, mosaics, silk, and glass. In their glorious days the Venetians lavishly used gold on objects as different as ship's cables and bars of foie gras, pastry, and bread. Gold was loved by all craftsmen for its richness, its suggestion of opulence. In sixteenth-century and seventeenth-century England and the European countries gold appeared on coaches, barges, plaster work, furniture, beads, wallpaper, leather, inn signs, and numerous other common objects. In the English house called Chatsworth the window frames were gilded both inside and outside.

In addition to its use in jewelry and in dental work, gold leaf has recently been found useful for patching punctured blood vessels and other damaged tissues. It adheres closely to most body tissue when it is electrically charged, which is done, as it has been done for centuries, by drawing the gilder's tip over the hair of one's head. "The adherence of the gold leaf, its malleability, chemical inertness and tensile strength," according to an article in *The Journal of the American Medical Association*, "renders gold leaf of singular value in surgery."

The art of beating gold is an ancient one, recorded as far back as Pliny's times. Because it is brilliant and durable and it can survive hard use and weather for so long, it is its own historian; and from existing examples the ancient practice of gold-beating may be studied. It was known to the Israelites, who may have learned it during their exile in Egypt, and to the Phoenicians. From India it spread to Korea, Japan, and then to China, where the gold-beaters made small quantities of leaves, sometimes singly, between black papers. Two beaters seated opposite to each other gave alternate blows to the thin metal.

Gold-beating by hand has now become a thing of the past, at least in

Figure 76: Sandwich-edge tray decorated with a landscape possibly painted by William Davis.

the Western hemisphere. Skilled gold-beaters learned the work as boys, but it is now difficult to find young men willing to learn such crafts, and a method has been developed for beating by electromagnetic hammer-blows, which are flexible enough to equal manual blows, thus saving hours of labor. Gold leaf comes in books with each thin square lying between rouge papers. The first quality, called bright, was made of the purest gold, and it was easily distinguished from the second quality, a low-carat gold by the color and the increased hardness. For this low-carat, gold was alloyed with copper or silver, which changed the shade to reddish or whitish, according to the metal used.

Gold formed an important part of the decoration on lacquered or japanned wares, and Bielefeld said there was good evidence that metal leaf continued untarnished longer on papier mâché than on any other substance. Notice that he used the term metal leaf, for true gold leaf never tarnishes. This affinity for using gold with black japan developed from love of the Oriental lacquer designs, which displayed gold and other metals used in leaf, powder, and flake forms, bright and dull, alone or in combination with colors and pearl shell. The English japanners imitated the work using their own methods. The best-quality gold leaf was used for the best japanned work, but in the nineteenth century second-quality was used as well as various substitutes. Often gold was not gold at all, but an alloy or silver washed with a gold varnish.

In working with the gold leaf, which was far too precious to be generally, and unprofitably, used, there was a certain amount of waste gold in the japan shops. The designs to be gilded could absorb only a certain amount of the gold sheet, and the excess was brushed off with cotton. The waste gold, called sweepings, was not at first saved, but swept into the streets. About 1758 one man became alert to the possible value of the waste gold and ingratiated himself with the workers, successfully persuading them to allow him to carry away the sweepings from the floor. In return he treated the men at Christmas. Eventually the japan masters also realized the value of the waste gold and collected the proceeds themselves. It then became the practice to collect all the cotton swabs used for gilding and to throw them into a special container. Then, at regular intervals, men from the gold-metal trade collected the waste material and extracted the gold by burning. The return from the reconstituted gold amounted to as much as six or seven pounds, and more, a year for a very large concern.

Some resplendent late-Victorian trays had speckles strewn over certain portions of a painted design. This gave a glittery effect somewhat like the simulated crystal snow on old Christmas cards. These speckles were usually made of gold leaf. To make them, a glass bottle was covered on the outside with the leaf and allowed to dry. The gold was then burnished with cotton and coated with varnish. The bottle was filled with cold water, and with a palette knife the gold was scraped off in fine crumbs for collection.

Prior to World War I pure gold powder was available in France. It was made from the best gold leaf by a tedious manual operation and was therefore more costly than bronze powder or false-gold powder. This pure gold powder was made in such lovely colors as *jaune, verte, citron,* and *rouge,* colors that were popular for the art of illumination. Bronze powders were known in the seventeenth and eighteenth centuries. At first they came largely from Germany, and these were considered the best, but some of the gold powder was made of brass and later turned to dirty green.

It was the American Henry Bessemer (1813–1898) who found a way to grind up metals and metallic ores in natural colors or stained by chemical means to make the powders in a variety of colors. The metals used for this purpose were brass, copper, zinc, silver, gold, and Dutch metal in various alloys.

Dutch metal, because it was inexpensive and had the brilliance of gold, became a widely used substitute for gold leaf and was especially in demand for such things as harness parts, coffin furniture, and kitchenwares. This product of Holland was an alloy of brass and copper that came in white or yellow "gold" foil. After the middle of the nineteenth century it was greatly reduced in price owing to its being admitted into England duty-free. At that time a book containing twenty-three hundred leaves, which had cost twelve shillings and six pence, was reduced to less than half that price.

There were four different kinds of Dutch bronze leaf: *common,* which was soft and reddish in color and made of one part zinc to three parts copper; *French,* which contained more zinc and was harder; *Florence,*

Figure 77: Papier-mâché tray in the Clay style, depicting the Muse of Poetry.

Figure 78: Detail of the center of the tray illustrated in *Figure* 77.

Figure 79: Large tray with a red center and free-hand bronze double border on black. *Figure 80:* Free-hand bronze papier-mâché small tray.

which was made of a still larger proportion of zinc and was greenish in color; and *white-leaf*, which was made of tin. All these provided a brilliant surface ornamentation for japanned metal goods, but they were not used extensively on papier-mâché wares.

In the seventeenth century a silvery leaf was used for gold by coating the metal with a yellow varnish, called "Golden Mecca," a mixture of shellac, gamboge, and dragon's blood dissolved in spirit. Several coats were applied over the silver design until the desired depth of gold was achieved. In 1775 gold varnish usually consisted of amber gum-lac, oil of turpentine, and an ingredient called hepatica aloe.

An example of the use of this imitation gold on a coach was recorded by Samuel Pepys (1633–1703). In 1669 he wanted to have his coach refurbished for May Day. The coach-maker offered to him a choice of gold or of treated silver, and Pepys resolved to have "this new sort of varnish." He watched the men, as they put several coats of golden varnish over the silver work, "which is pretty to see how every doing it over makes it more yellow, . . ." and "it is very pretty when well laid on and not too pale as some are even to show the silver."

It is to John Evelyn (1620–1706) that credit must be given for introducing an inexpensive varnish that imitated gold color. Whether the idea was originated with Evelyn, or whether he had knowledge of the Chinese treatment of joss papers, is not known; but in the Orient the tin foil on ceremonial papers and sacrificial offerings was treated in a similar manner. Small squares of tin foil were pasted to paper and were then brushed over with a yellow liquid made from a gluey extraction from seaweed or were dyed with a solution made from the flower of the pagoda tree (*Sophora Japanica*), either of which gave the tin a golden appearance. This treatment of the silver, to give it the appearance of gold, was also used at the eighteenth-century Pontypool Japan Works and in the Midlands industries until World War I.

Although all white metal, foil, or powder was called silver, it was really tin or an alloy with tin or zinc. True silver leaf turns brown when varnished and continues to darken with time. In his famous treatise *Il Libro dell'Arte* (*c.* 1400) Cennino Cennini gave the following advice on this phenomenon: "Know that above all you are to work with as little silver as you can because it does not last; it turns black. . . . Use beaten tin or tin foil instead of it henceforth. Also beware of alloyed gold for it sometimes turns black." To avoid this discoloration, it was necessary to use isinglass in water, filtered with a little spirit of wine, a tablespoon to two cups of isinglass solution, according to Wedgwood's *Common Book.* But even that mixture darkened in time. With much less trouble better results were obtained by using tin foil or white Dutch metal until other white metals were discovered.

One of these metals was paladium of the platinum family, which was discovered in 1803, but was at that time far too costly for the japanning trade. Aluminum was a suitable substitute for silver, but it was not available until 1830; and it remained too costly until after 1864, when some changes in the preparation of the powder form by Clair Deville made it sufficiently inexpensive for japan ornament. There was as well the fictitious silver powder known in the early days as "Argentium Musivium."

To ornament with gold leaf or other metal leaf is not for the inexperienced, but a brief account of the general method should be given. First, the article should be well sanded and completely dry. Then the surface should be dusted with talcum powder or cornstarch so that no damp or sticky spots remain to catch the gold leaf. With a hard pencil the design is then traced on the object, using graphite paper or tracing paper rubbed with chalk or magnesium powder. Then with a small quill brush and enamel or varnish mixed with paint or gold bronze powder, a portion of the design is painted and allowed to stand until nearly dry, when it feels tacky to the touch, but does not come off. The gold leaf is then laid on the painted design, the excess being brushed off with cotton wool or velvet. Occasionally some spots will seem too dry to take the leaf, and these areas may be breathed on, a procedure that will help the leaf to cling. The rest of the design is accomplished in the same way until the entire object is covered with the gold leaf, which must then be allowed to harden for several days. Finally, the whole is polished with cotton wool.

Figure 81: Late nineteenth-century match-holder of papier-mâché with gilt figures and painted faces and hands.

99

Mother of Pearl

Pearl Fisheries near this place, TUTECORUN, is the famous fishery whereof there are no more than three in the east, viz. 1, near ORMUS: 2, Bay of AINAM on the Chinese coast and 3 in the Bay between Cape Comoryn and the Isle of CEYLON wherein are also comprehended MANAAR and ARIPON. The pearls are found in certain 'Oister' shells (which are not good to eat) and are taken by diving, 7, 8, 9 or 10 fathom deep, sometimes not without great danger. Abundance of pearl dust is from hence transported into Europe where it is used in cordial medicines.—'A True and Exact Description of the Most Celebrated East Indian Coast of Malabar and Coromandel and Ceylon', from Coromandel India, 1618.

FROM earliest times, the form and color of sea shells have so fascinated man that he has used them for many decorative and practical purposes. They have served as a form of currency, the cowrie having been one of the earliest means of exchange. The purple and white clam shells from which the American Indians made wampum were similarly used, the purple shell having the greater value. The spiky murex was important for the making of purple dye and a permanent color known as Tyrian purple, which was used to illuminate manuscripts. Since late Roman times monks have carved pilgrim souvenirs from the shell of the great pearl oyster in the form of crucifixes, wafer boxes, and beads. Primitive peoples used large conch shells as horns and bivalves for utensils.

Lady Mary Wortley Montagu's letters from Turkey tell of the many extravagant uses of mother of pearl in fine Turkish residences. In a letter of 1718, she described a lavish room in the Sultan's palace with wainscotting of mother of pearl "fasten'd with Emeralds like nails."

In England shell grottoes were a popular feature of gardens, and ladies practiced for a long time the handicraft called shell-work, which consisted of gluing small colorful shells onto picture frames, boxes, and similar objects.

An Elizabethan remedy for fever—for the rich—was made of powdered pearls and lemon juice, according to Burton. For this purpose an

Figure 82: Round papier-mâché dish, in the rear, and a papier-mâché calendar. These two pieces are examples of late, commercially ornamented papier-mâché products, with the faces and hands of the figures embossed, probably late nineteenth-century or early twentieth-century.

Figure 83: Tray decorated with a painting of Warwick Castle on the Avon, framed in broken pearl with a gold border.

Figure 84: Table decorated with a representation of Tintern Abbey in pearl. The pearl is used to simulate stone work; the sky was done in bronze powder. The pedestal is moulded.

abundance of pearl dust was shipped to England from pearl fisheries on the China coast, in Ceylon, and on the Persian Gulf coast. In the nineteenth century a similar concoction made of the residue scrap nacre from the pearl-grinding industry was used as a cosmetic wash. The nacre was ground to a fine powder, mixed with lemon juice, and allowed to stand for a day or two, after which it was filtered, bottled, and sold. As recently as 1952, the famous pearl-dealer Kokichi Mikimoto, at the age of ninety-two, averred that he owed his "fine health and long life to the two pearls I have swallowed every morning since I was twenty."

Perhaps the most interesting use of shell and certainly the most decorative was the pearl inlay with which the Chinese, Koreans, and Japanese enhanced their lacquer work. The finest Chinese shell-work was the exquisitely carved inlay produced by a method unknown to Western pearl-workers. An exceptionally fine example is an eight-fold screen completely and realistically ornamented with carved white pearl oyster shell, on which every bird feather is a separate piece, as are the tree trunks, foliage, and flowers, all glimmering on black lacquer (*Figure 85*).

The shimmering nacre of the smooth inner lining of the shell was the most valuable part, other than the pearl itself, for ornamenting japanned and lacquered articles. This iridescent lining of the sea shell was built up of layers of nacre formed annually. The greatest demand for decorative use was for the white nacre of the great pearl oyster, the inedible *margaritifera*, which also yielded the choicest pearls. This oyster is found in the waters of the Persian Gulf, of the Arabian Sea, of the Indian Ocean, and around the Philippine Islands.

The true pearl takes form in a sac when a tiny grain of sand or other foreign body serves as a nucleus around which layers of nacre mother the foreign irritant, eventually producing a pearl. The Chinese knew about this process, for even early in the thirteenth century they were placing small metal forms, usually of a Buddha, inside mussel shells (*mya margaritifera*), which then became coated with nacre and made highly valued little charms. In similar fashion the famous Mikimoto industry produced cultured pearls using the pearl oyster.

At first, the shells discarded after the pearls had been removed were used for ballast in the East Indiamen returning to Europe from the Orient,

Figure 85: Screen of black lacquered papier mâché entirely ornamented with exquisitely carved shell, a superb example of Chinese pearl work.

Figure 86: Early seventeenth-century English cabinet of wood, decorated with mother of pearl and paint in the same fashion as later papier-mâché pieces were decorated.

and in 1696 pearl shell was one of a number of East Indian commodities offered for sale in England and Holland. In that century shell was used, perhaps in limited amounts, on furniture. In *Figure 86* is illustrated a seventeenth-century English cabinet of wood ornamented with paint and mother of pearl.

In the trade, the shell was known by the name of the point from which it was shipped, for example, Bombay pearl, Panama pearl, or Egyptian shells, the latter sent from the Red Sea to Alexandria. Other types were known by their color, as black-edged, yellow-edged, red, and green. After 1840 the Panamanian fisheries supplied the market, and a decade later Australia was exporting shell.

By the end of the nineteenth century schooners were used as floating stations in Australian waters. Nine of these schooners, of from 69 to 132 tons, were located off the Thursday Islands. These floating stations as well as the pearling boats from which the divers worked were required to pay a high license fee. Tenders worked between the stations and the shore, and eventually the shell harvest went to Sydney to be shipped from there. In earlier days, when the shell was more plentiful, the industry was quite profitable, but many of the fisheries soon became exhausted, making it necessary to go farther afield and to permit the overfished section to rest.

The choicest shells were packed in cases for shipping, but the Japanese ear shells were shipped loose in ton lots or in bags. The nacre that had been ground into flakes or leaves by the English pearl-workers for commercial use was shipped in kegs to America and other countries. During the peak of the popularity of mother of pearl, roughly from 1830 to 1850, twenty-five hundred tons of shell were offered for sale in London in a single year, and in 1872 the English imports were from five hundred to two thousand tons.

One hundredweight of the best quality shell brought from ten to twelve shillings, and of the ordinary grades as little as three shillings. The shells of the pearl oyster and the abalone, when flattened, sold for a little over two shillings an ounce; and plain white shell, some of which came from Australia, sold for a little less.

The button industry used the largest quantity of shell in the nineteenth century, and fancy Victorian objects, such as cutlery, cane handles, card cases, fan sticks, buckles, and fish game counters, ran second. The fish counters—mother of pearl carved in the form of fish—were used for Loo, an eighteenth-century parlor game. The name was derived from the French *fiche*. For these things and the thin nacre veneer used on boxes and tea caddies, the lovely, rippling white pearl oyster was needed in large quantities.

Robson's Directory for 1839 divides the pearl trade into five sections: shell dealers, blank-makers, ornament-makers, setters, and manufacturers. In 1852 there were only twenty-three names under the heading of pearl-ornament workers, and after 1863 none was listed.

The japanning industry also used large quantities of shell, but the amount used of the tons imported is hard to determine. The japanners used several types of nacre, but favored the rainbow colors, the prismatic shades of the wrinkled aurora, and the green and blue of the ear shell, especially for floral designs. The black or South Sea shell had a deep, dark iridescence. It was considered of little value at first, and piles of this shell were buried in the ground at Birmingham. Later in the century, during the 1870s, smoked pearl buttons became fashionable for coats and vests, and demand raised the price so that the buried shell was uncovered, removed, and used.

In connection with this activity, a story is told about a Birmingham workman who volunteered to dig up his neighbor's yard without charge. Naturally his offer was not accepted. The man persisted in his efforts and offered to give five pounds to the owner and in addition to carry away the rubbish. Permission was finally given and the "rubbish," which proved to be discarded pearl shell, was dug up and carted away and sold for twenty pounds. This same man, we are told, said that the Birmingham Town Hall (shown depicted in mother of pearl and gold on a plaque in *Figure 87*) was built on such mounds of shell that it would almost pay to pull it down at today's prices for the sake of the shell obtained. The Birmingham Town Hall is a solidly built stone structure, erected in 1834, and it would be interesting to learn if that much shell had been discarded before 1834, when the papier-mâché industry was at its height.

In the early days of the industry, before shell was used in such enormous quantities, boys were employed to file and grind the nacre by hand

Figure 87: Plaque, *c.* 1850, depicting Birmingham Town Hall in a mother-of-pearl decoration on papier mâché, with gilding.

Figure 88: Detail of a tray center with painted and pearl flowers. *Figure 89:* Detail of another tray center with painted and pearl flowers.

to a proper thinness, which was 1/40 to 1/100 of an inch. This was slow and tedious work as well as unhealthy, and many young people consequently suffered from a form of silicosis caused by the inhalation of shell dust. Finally, manual filing was replaced by the use of the horizontal grinding wheel. With the palm of the hand protected by a piece of corduroy, the worker held the shell flat against the wheel until it was ground so thin that care was required in handling it. The flakes were then cut into shapes with a knife or a pair of scissors after the brittle shell had been softened in hot water. Broken fragments were used for hit-or-miss borders or for flower buds or other tiny figures.

Henry Clay patented a type of pearl decoration for papier mâché in 1778, probably for buttons. Existing examples of his early products with mother-of-pearl decoration are rare. The King Gothic tray illustrated in *Figure 74,* which is stamped on the back "Clay, King St., Covent Garden," has carefully cut shell in the forms of Chinese figures, boats, birds, pagodas, and many varieties of tree foliage.

George Souter, an employee at Jennens & Bettridge, conceived of shaping the pearl flakes with acid and patented the process in 1825. The method was to draw the desired shape on the thin pearl flake, a flower, a leaf, a petal, a heart or something similar. The shell was next coated with varnish within the outline of the tracing and allowed to dry. Then hydrochloric acid or nitric acid was brushed over the varnished shell, causing it to bubble and dance and to turn faintly yellow. For a brief time fumes of carbon dioxide and free chlorine rose as the acid contacted the shell. After one or two applications of the acid, the superfluous portion disappeared leaving the desired shape intact. Any rough edges could be carefully filed or sanded smooth. This method guaranteed less breakage.[1]

New developments were often the result of evading a rival's patent. One such attempt was made by Woodward and Midgeley of Birmingham, when they tried gluing the shell flakes to thin sheet copper and then marking the outline of the motif on the mounted shell. It was then sent to the

---

[1] The author tried shaping a pearl flake with hydrochloric acid and was successful in forming a basic flower shape. The acid can be purchased at a drugstore. Cutting the pearl flake with a pair of small scissors, after the shell has been soaked in warm water, is probably the easier way.

"saw-piercers" to be cut out. This idea proved to be impractical, and it was given up.

When a quantity of mother of pearl in shapes all of the same size was needed, such as stars, diamonds, and serpentines for borders, the pearl flakes were stacked and lightly cemented between each flake, the outline of the motif being drawn on the topmost piece. The pile was then cut as one with a press tool adapted in such a way as to evade Souter's patent or with a file, and the cemented stack was then thrown into warm water, which dissolved the cement and separated the pieces—all then alike.

If a piece of mother of pearl is missing from a design on papier mâché, it leaves a shallow cavity (*Figure 89*), giving the impression that the shell had been inlaid, but the cavity was actually caused by the layering of black japan, built up to the surface of the shell. It was done in the following manner. A coat of size was first applied to the blank article. Before it was dry, the shell shapes were placed in the spots desired by the pearler, who picked up the bits of shell on the point of a stick dipped in size. When all the pieces were properly placed, the article was taken to the blacking room where it received several coats of black japan, each coat being thoroughly stove-dried before the next was added. Finally, the surface of the article was rubbed with pumice until the black was removed from the mother of pearl and the surface was level. After more polishing, the artist could complete the design with paint or gold leaf.

In most of the floral designs, in which mother of pearl was used, some of the flowers may be entirely of paint; the others, in the design of shell. Or, perhaps, a painted flower had a small spot of shell in the center, on which were painted stamens and pistil. Sometimes foliage and stems were painted with one or two leaves of mother of pearl added for interest and contrast. On the die-stamped card tray illustrated in *Figure 90*, the flowers are placed in a cornucopia-shaped vase and are of colorful aurora and white pearl oyster shell, although the paint has almost disappeared from the surface. The parlor-maid's tray, sometimes called a "kidney tray," illustrated in *Figure 72*, is an example of the best work with its small well shaped vase and carefully cut roses and other figures. The design covers the tray, yet it is light, delicate and tasteful.

For coloring the surface of mother of pearl, transparent paints were

Figure 90: Tray decorated with rippling abalone shell and plain white shell.
Figure 91: Decorated glass inset for the portable desk illustrated in *Figure 149.*

used, and these often added beauty to the natural shell, which glowed through the paint. Opaque paints were used for stamens, petal folds, sepals, and other accents and details, and sometimes opaque green was put onto a pearl leaf. Because the shell surface was slick, the paint often wore off, but the exposed shell was not unattractive.

Abbeys, bridges, ruins, and towers were sometimes depicted in carefully selected pearl slabs placed so that the ripple of the nacre adds perspective and gives the effect of stone blocks (*Figure 84*). The color was sometimes matched in order to have a pink reflection on one side and a green on the other. A white nacre with a grain or ripple was used either alone or with transparent color over it. In other painted buildings the pearl shell may have been placed to produce a reflection as if from a sunset or bright sky.

Pearl shell was also used on painted glass panels, which were first used with papier mâché by Thomas Lane of Great Hampton Street in Birmingham in 1849 (*Figure 91*). To paint on glass in reverse, the artist starts with the foremost details in the picture and works backwards to the sky, which is last. For example, to paint a country cottage, the window and door frames or roof details would be put in first as well as any flowers or shrubbery in front of the building. When they are dry, the solid parts of the windows, curtains, shades, or panes, the door, the roof, and the cottage walls would be next, and finally the sky. The section in which the pearl was to be placed was left plain, unless there were a few small details such as textured lines of stone, which would be added before the shell was attached with varnish or size.

Papier-mâché pieces from which the shell shapes have been lost can be repaired quite easily with thin pearl flakes or "leaves," which can be purchased at art-supply stores. A tracing of the vacant space to be filled must first be made. Then the outline is traced onto the shell with carbon paper. The shell must be soaked in hot water, and, when it is soft enough, it may be cut with a pair of small scissors. The shell shape is then placed in the vacant area with Elmer's glue or any other good adhesive and permitted to dry. The vacant area may need to be filled if it is quite deep and the shell too thin. It can be filled with the glue until it is near enough to the top edge. When the glue is set, the shell is laid onto it.

Another product of the sea from the East and Australia was tortoise shell, which was often used as an inlay or a veneer with mother of pearl. The japan shops, however, used only an imitation of tortoise shell, achieved by putting black japan over a fiery red, usually silver leaf that had been coated with alizarin crimson. The black paint was then lifted off the red with a crumpled cloth or dry brush, leaving irregular mottled patches resembling tortoise shell. Later vermilion paint was used under black, substituted for the more expensive silver leaf.

The Ornamenters

Use Coloquintido with Gum Arabick and sugar to keep the Flies from soiling your Work if it shall be exposed.—The Method of Learning to Draw in Perspective, by J. Peele, 1735.

The quality of the ornament was a matter hardly considered ... indeed all goods was barbarous in the extreme ... but much has been gained by the introduction of pearl as an adjunct to the pencil.—The Birmingham and General Advertiser, 1847.

JAPANNED wares had upon "their varied productions, ornament of some kind or other. Quality was hardly considered but ornament was indispensible." This point of view published in *The Birmingham and General Advertiser* in 1847 was not altogether true, for some of the better firms saw to it that their artists received some training. It is well to remember that the "good taste" of one hundred years ago was rather less restrained than it is today, but even so the manufacturers knew "the errors of the style preferred" for papier-mâché decoration, and as long as the popular taste was for show and glitter and sales remained high, it would have been too much to expect the manufacturers to change that style.

Of course, a certain amount of poor and naïve workmanship was turned out, but it is certain that it did not originate in a firm with high standards. The ornament on the majority of products, whether one likes the design or not, was well executed—good brushwork in the painting and gilding and a smooth application of bronze powders, experienced work in whatever medium was used. It is also possible to find a tray on which two or three persons had a hand in the decoration, noticeable because a flower or the foliage is less convincing than the rest of the design. This could have been the work of a trainee, a young man who had been through several weeks of learning to use the camel's-hair pencil or brush. It takes more than a few weeks to acquire freedom and ease with a brush, unless the person is very gifted.

Young men wishing to learn to do the fine brushwork were put through a rigorous course. His beginner's brushstrokes were repeatedly criticized by the foreman and then wiped out and done again until he acquired perfect skill with the brush. When his brushwork was satisfactory, he was permitted to try his hand at "sprigging" (*Figure 92*), which consisted in painting small flowers, foliage, and butterflies with gold size and then gilding them. Later veins, petals, and stamens were "scratched in" or etched on the surface of the gold leaf. Having developed skill in these techniques, if he chose, the young man could learn the work of pearling.

Not all japanner-painters had been trained from youth in the tinware and papier-mâché shops. Many had come from the coachmaking trade, where they had painted heraldic devices and other gilded ornaments onto the japanned coach bodies. Others had ornamented furniture or earthenware and porcelain, for experienced industrial painters could easily transfer their brushwork to the japanned wares. A japanner was equally at home working on paper, wood, or metal, because apart from the basic material there was no difference in the work.

The ornamenters sat at long tables placed in front of the windows that lined the side of the room. Each man was equipped with a palette knife, camel's-hair brushes, tins and cups of turpentine and varnish, and a square stone or marble and muller for mixing pigment and oil. The best stones were of marble, spotted granite, or any good close-grained stone so that the pigment could not be caught in the cracks or pores. A muller was a somewhat egg-shaped piece of porphyry, marble, or other polished stone about five inches long with a flat, smooth working end that measured two or three inches across. It was used for mixing the pigment and oil in the

Figure 92: Examples of sprigging.

hollow of the marble as a pestle and mortar are used. The painter put a little linseed oil and powdered pigment on the marble, and with the muller or a soft-bladed knife mixed the two ingredients well, then lifted the mixed paint to his palette.

In London, from about 1746, horse mills were used for grinding paint until improved methods were adopted. The pigment was then put into small bladders, which sold for three pence a groat (size of a hull barley kernel) or six pence a piece, according to the quality or value of the pigment. To use the paint packaged in this way the artist pricked the bladder to remove a small amount, though if the paint were not used up rapidly it would dry out. It was therefore more economical to mix what was needed in the marble. Later, for artist's colors in collapsible tubes, patented by John Rand of New York City in 1850, tubes of pure tin were introduced for substances contaminated by lead, according to *Tin through the Ages* by Flower.

A small number of men became sufficiently good artists to enter the academic field and to exhibit at the Royal Academy. One was Edward Bird (1772–1819), a self-taught artist who was elected to the Royal Academy in 1817. Bird had been apprenticed at the Old Hall Works when he was thirteen, and, according to George Wallis, who also painted at the Old Hall, at eighteen Bird was painting tray centers in the style of Gainsborough and later "excelled in Shakespearean compositions and depicted scenes from Don Quixote and Hudibras." The panel shown in *Figure 93* may be a copy of Giorgioni's *The Tempest* or *Rest on The Flight*, or perhaps an adaptation from Wheatley; it is attributed to Edward Bird.

There is a story about Bird that, when he and several companions were visiting in Boulogne, they were served tea on a beautiful tray, which excited his friends' notice and praise. They remarked that they did not think such things could have been made in France. Bird looked at the tray, smiled, and said: "It was not made here . . . for I painted it."

George Wallis (1811–1891) specialized in landscapes and while working for Ryton and Walton at the Old Hall designed a sheet-iron tray that he called the "Victoria" in honor of the young queen. It was oval with a scalloped edge and was made in a nest of four or five sizes. Wallis worked at the Old Hall from 1827 until 1832, when he left to go to Manchester for further study. He eventually became artist-commissioner of the great Exhibition and the First Keeper of the South Kensington Museum.

Joseph Barney (1751–1827) was a fruit-and-flower painter to the Prince Regent. At sixteen he left Wolverhampton to study under Zucchi and Angelica Kauffmann, who had come to London from Rome in 1766. In 1774 Barney won a premium at the Society of Arts, and he exhibited his classical and scriptural subjects at the Royal Academy in 1786. After twenty-seven years as drawing master at the Royal Military Academy in Woolwich, Barney returned to Wolverhampton to paint trays for his brother, a partner in the firm of Bevins and Barney. In 1791 he established a studio where he employed artists to decorate blanks for other japanneries. Barney is also remembered for the murals of scriptural subjects that he painted in Staffordshire churches.

Another painter was William Davis who joined Walton's in 1842. Two bronze pictures, *The Goddess of Earth* and *Daniel in the Lion's Den*, are attributed to him. He became an expert in copying Morland's rustic scenes on trays of good quality, and he originated patterns of rural subjects for other japanner-painters to copy. For some years after 1850 he was working for McCallum and Hodson.

From the earliest time of the industry many well known paintings and engravings were copied on japanned articles. *The Aurora*, *The Tempest*, and Morland's work have been mentioned, and there were others by Landseer, Stubbs, Sandby, Alken, and Kauffmann. With truth *The Birmingham and General Advertiser* stated in 1847: "In copying scenes from the painted and engraved works of artists, the name of the artist is omitted. Now this should not be . . . in no case should this appropriation be made without acknowledgement."

The widespread use of an artist's work without credit to him was to a large extent stopped by law with the passage of an *Act to Consolidate and Amend the Laws relating to the Copyright of Designs for ornamenting Articles of Manufacture*. One result of this act was that many ornamenters of japanned ware changed the designs commonly used. Copies of famous paintings and popular prints were simply no longer made, and their designs became floral or depictive of primitive landscapes, banal ideas safe from the laws of copyright. In 1842 the government issued registration marks for use on goods made of metal, wood, glass, and ceramics, marks consisting of Roman numerals to indicate the material and capital letters to indicate the year and the month of manufacture. These marks and variations of them continued in use until 1883, although they are very rarely found on japanned tinplate or papier mâché.

Allegorical subjects, such as the muses of poetry (*Figures 77 & 78*) and music, were popular in bronze, as were patriotic subjects. The victories of Trafalgar and Waterloo brought a wave of patriotism that was reflected in the work of the painters. For example, pictured on one panel is a confident, triumphant Brittania riding in Neptune's chariot and carrying Neptune's trident and a shield covered with the Union Jack. The picture was executed in bronze powders and paint at the shop of Illidge and Company of Wolverhampton about 1818, and was displayed at an exhibition of papier mâché at the Royal Society of Arts in September of 1921.

Borders alone were used on tray galleries and rims in the late Georgian period, and their use evolved from the seventeenth-century and eighteenth-century coach-painter's practice of combining simple borders with armorial bearings and crests on the bodies of vehicles. Early borders consisted of running vines, berries, flowers and foliage, simple scrolls, and brushstrokes. Later the borders became rococo in style with C-shaped and S-shaped scrolls, arabesques, cartouches with cross-hatching, sprigs, medallions, swastika frets, and Greek key, often with such space-fillers added as small curlicues, ovals, and circles in varying sizes, repeated stars (called *œil de perdrix*) (*Figure 94*), and the fine meandering lines of Pontypool fame known as Stormont work (*Figure 95*). On some late fancy Gothic trays there were fine lines, clustered and hanging straight, dripped like fine icicles from a lacy border, with many of the drips reaching into the floor of the tray. These border motifs can be seen on French and Worcester porcelain, from which they were undoubtedly copied. All is fair in business, for the potteries also borrowed ideas from the japanneries. The delicate gold borders were done with a fine sable brush wielded with the ease of long training.

Bordering was at one time even a separate branch of the trade and was performed by men who made a specialty of this part of decorating. The borderers were considered ordinary workers, not artists, because the work

Figure 93: A tinplate panel with a painting attributed to Edward Bird, R. A.
Figure 94: Green game-counter tray with a chinoiserie design in gold. Notice
the filler on the border of *œil de perdrix*. *Figure 95:* Travellers' examples of
patterns for tinware snuffer trays. Notice the pattern on the left, which shows
Stormont work.

was more mechanical than landscape painting, an unfair point of view really, for bordering is an exacting work, requiring more precision and brush control than painting a group of flowers. As the industry became more productive, transfer-printing was introduced, and with constant improvement, it eventually replaced the handiwork of the brushwork borderer.

Transfer-printing was a form of decoration used in the potteries, and had been first introduced in 1752 by Sadler and Green, tile-makers of Liverpool. The process began with an accurate drawing of the design carefully planned to fit the contour of the article to which it was to be applied. This drawing was then given to the engraver, who cut the design into copper plate, which was coated with an especial ink. An impression was taken from the copper onto a thin paper. The paper was then laid with the inked side down on the article, rubbed with a hard brush or similar tool, and removed after a few minutes, leaving the design transferred onto the surface of the piece.

Stephen Bedford, of varnish fame, obtained a patent in 1759 for "impressing in imitation of engraving upon varnish laid upon copper, iron, paper and other bodies to be used on coach panels, snuff boxes and other kinds of merchandise, impressions of foliage, decorative ornaments and other devices." This appears to be the first use of transfer-printing for japanned objects, and it was undoubtedly Bedford's method that was used by John Taylor for Lady Shelburne's box. Although Bedford's patent did not prove entirely practical, it was based on the correct principle, and in time the method was further developed and finally perfected in 1809 by Charles Valentine of Clerkenwell. In 1852 George Goodman, who had worked for Alsager & Neville, patented a method for "ornamenting japanned wares by transferring thereto designs printed upon paper; the said designs being painted in oil colors from engraved plates." Goodman was working for Ebenezer Sheldon in the 1880s on a part-time basis, and in the Sheldon shop transferred designs were used on a "stone coloured background" (*Figures 96 & 97*).

The method of transferring a gold-leaf design was to cover the entire surface of the article with gold leaf laid on a gelatin size. The design was next transferred with a mixture of printer's ink and wax, and then the

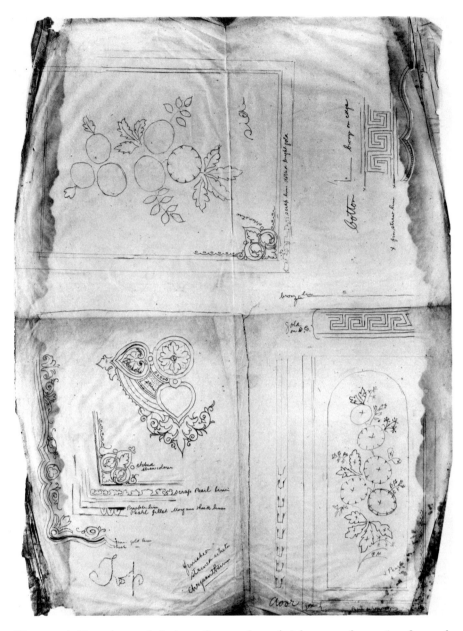

Figure 96: Drawings of designs for papier-mâché wares from the firm of Ebenezer Sheldon. The cabinet design with sprays of chrysanthemums in straw-colored gold and white is perhaps the work of Elgin.

Figure 97: Transfer pattern combining a Greek key and amalakas in a circular design. The amalaka was a bulbous or melon-like ornament often used to terminate the shikaras of medieval India. Notice at the outer edge a somewhat angular Hepplewhite brushstroke border.

whole piece was covered with black varnish in the same way that mother of pearl was covered over. When the varnish was dry, the printer's ink and wax were removed by warmth and friction and with it the black varnish, revealing the gold design. In this method, where so much gold was covered over with black, the metal leaf used was undoubtedly the inexpensive Dutch metal. Transfer-printing eliminated the work of the borderer. The same design could be used repeatedly for an article of the same shape, as, for example, the bellows and pattern shown in *Figures 98 & 99*.

Flowers have always been a popular subject for decorators. On japanned wares they were portrayed in metal leaf, bronze powders, pigment, and pearl. Subjects were taken from chintzes, engravings, earthenware, and nature, as the vagaries of the British climate produced beautiful examples in gardens large and small that served as models. Of course, the rose was a favorite; others in wide use were tulips, camelias, single dahlias, poppies, irises, pinks, primulas, morning glories, and fuchsias. They were often combined with sprays of hawthorne, forget-me-nots, lily of the valley, harebells, broom, grasses, and all kinds of foliage.

In the mid-Victorian period, many King and Queen Gothic trays were given a bronze ground that faded out at the edges into the black background or, more rarely, were covered with gold powder to the edge of the tray. In order to do this, the tray was coated with varnish, and when it was nearly dry, the gold powder was rubbed lightly into it, always the japanner's method, not by first mixing the powder with size, which would have been a gold paint. The designs were then painted onto the gold ground.

A few who specialized in painting flowers are always remembered and always mentioned in any work on papier mâché. One was Richard Steele of Wolverhampton, who left the potteries to paint japanned wares; he was an excellent painter. At the Municipal Gallery in Wolverhampton a large flower-filled panel of his work is on display.

Actually, there were many instances of apparent coöperation between manufacturers of earthenware and ceramics and the japanneries in exchanging both designs and painters. The Willow pattern is perhaps the best known among these designs. According to Geoffrey Godden, in an article published in *Connoisseur*, the Worcester porcelain dealers accommodated their customers by offering japanned papier-mâché tea trays with the same design as that used on their china.

Luke Amner, who worked in many shops, specialized in tulips, and William Bourne painted verbenas for Walton. Jackson liked to paint lily of the valley, and Alfred Harvey slowly and painstakingly painted flowers of many sorts, often rubbing one out and painting it again. Edward Haselar, who lived to the age of ninety, worked for Jennens and Bettridge from 1832 to 1845 or 1846, leaving then to work at Frederick Walton and Company. Walton was at that time searching out the best talent in the country. Haselar was believed by some to have brought realism in flower-painting on papier mâché.

The McCallum brothers, Philip and James, were both flower-painters, but Philip's work was considered superior. William Wylie and a great many others now long since forgot were flower-painters as well, and, of course, could paint other subjects too.

There was George Neville (1810–1887) whose work is usually described as painting "on the black." This was literally true, for he used the black ground as a base for his flowers, beginning with clear varnish and then pulling the dry pigment into the wet varnish, always carefully modelling the flower with a brush. The clear varnish on the black ground gave depth to the heart of the flower as well as to the narrow spaces between the petals (*Figure 68*). Flowers painted in clear wet varnish were softer in appearance than those painted in the straight manner, because the pigment softened and "floated" the color a little as the varnish dried.

The usual method for painting a flower was to make a base of a solid color, white, yellow, or whatever was suitable for the type of flower. When the base was dry, varnish with a little transparent paint was floated over it, and immediately the pigment was pulled into the wet varnish with a dry brush. Details were added later. Some flowers could be painted in two steps, though others might require three or four. The next-to-last step would be veiling or the application of petals in thin ghostly white paint. The last step would be putting in the fine lines for the stamen and dots and other small accents.

The simplest flower to paint is the morning glory, which was made on a round or oval white base. When dry, the varnish is washed over the

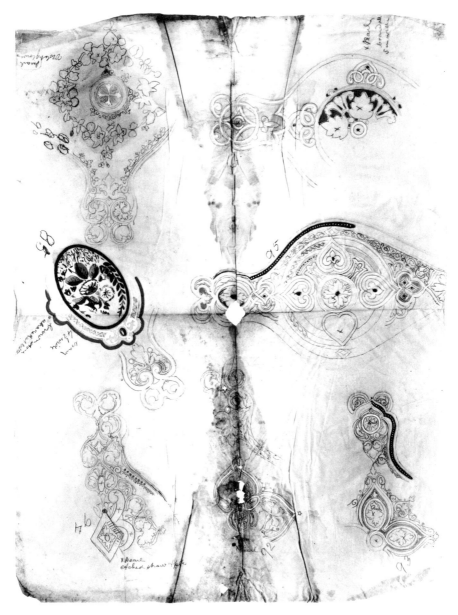

Figure 98: Bellows patterns with some color notes from the firm of Ebenezer Sheldon.

127

Figure 99: Bellows, two spectacle cases, and a card case.

base, and a touch of transparent yellow is placed in the center. With a dry brush and Prussian blue the color is pulled into the wet varnish from the outer edge, fading the blue just at the yellow center. If the edge of the yellow turns slightly green, there is no harm done, and it is sometimes effective. As the blue is being added, the brush should be wiped from time to time to remove the excess varnish that accumulated as the blue was added. Later, the pale alizarin ribs of the morning-glory petals are added with a fine brush, and in the center a small black stamen or two are put onto the yellow.

Birds were popular in flower groups and were often perched precariously on fragile stems or fountains. Fabulous birds, which George Neville liked to add to his designs, had gold-leaf bodies that shimmered under transparent colors and long filmy white tails, dreamily transparent except for some heavy white streamers for emphasis. Occasionally a bird's nest, complete with three eggs, was a part of the picture. In addition, there might be a wine-glass-shaped fountain of gold with water splashing over the sides and bugs or butterflies hovering in black areas.

THE CHINESE STYLE OR THE OLD INDIAN WORK

Chinese designs were a specialty of Joseph Booth and Edwin Booth, who may have been related, and, strangely, such designs had not been used to any extent in the Midlands industries until they were introduced in the 1820s by the Booths. "Chippendale's Chinese flirtings" as Howard Spring called chinoiseries, were used in the Pontypool japan works in the eighteenth century, but those designs were somewhat daintier and less stiff than the work of either of the Booths. Edwin was famous for his fine pen-work combined with raised figures, and in 1824 he decorated a tray in this manner for George IV. Joseph worked at Jennens & Bettridges from 1821 until 1835, and Edwin worked at Walton's. W. H. Jones in his book *Story of the Japan and Tinplate Trade* (1900) states erroneously that Edwin Booth was the father of Wilkes Booth, who assassinated President Lincoln, but a study of the Booth family history disproves this story. The actor Edwin Booth was born in Maryland in 1833, the son of Junius Brutus

Booth, and Wilkes Booth, the assassin, was another son of Junius Brutus and Edward's brother.

Chinese patterns were popular on earthenware, the best known being the willowware pattern. J. Peele, often quoted in these pages, stated that "the best figures to represent China [on japanned wares] may be taken from Tea Cups or from saucers and other pieces of Chinaware. But we might paint Coats of Arms in all their colors or any other device."

Booth's designs were formal and conventional in the manner of the willow pattern, not the light frivolous chinoiseries of the French rococo artists. The raised portions were made of whiting and varnish in a mixture somewhat firmer than creamy and were laid onto the drawn figure carefully and moulded with various small sticks or modelling tools. When dry, these raised figures were covered with bronze or with metal leaf, but the faces and hands were painted white or pink. They turned creamy with the final varnishings. When the "Indian Flowers" or peonies were used, the details were painted in color on white (*Figure 70*).

Most of the Chinese designs, as interpreted by the japanners, were known as "old Indian work." These consisted of stiff little islands suspended between small bodies of water, in which dainty boats were placed. Each bit of land was connected by an arched bridge or by a vague series of steps reaching up like Jacob's ladder to touch an island above. Rocks were portrayed in a variety of shapes, with grasses and bamboo here and there to soften the picture, as did the trees with dripping or fluffy foliage. Distant birds in flight were added by a repeated twist of a quill brush. Most of the Chinese ornaments, embossed or plain was worked mainly in metallic colors (*Figure 71*).

In the waning period of the industry the embossed areas on the transferred or printed designs were blobs of gesso, which served for the face and hands of the figures. The gesso was then painted white, and the features, hair, and fingers were indicated with fine black lines.

To Alsager, when he was working at Jennens, are attributed the clusters of Oriental towers and temples represented in gold and pearl slabs, with palm trees of pearl fronds. One of the rare Chinese designs composed of carefully cut pearl shapes and gold is signed "Clay."

FREE-HAND BRONZE OR WOLVERHAMPTON STYLE

An effective type of decoration that caught on well and was used over a long period was called free-hand bronze work, to distinguish it from bronze stencilling. It consisted of the application of bronze powders on a not quite dry enamelled design. The worker had near him a shallow tray, in which were cavities about the size of half an egg shell. In each cavity was a different shade of bronze powder. These powders were applied to the design by swabs or "bobs" with which the motifs were moulded and shaded.

The procedure was to paint on a dry surface with pigment, usually lamp black mixed with varnish. The paint and varnish are what we now call enamel. When this glossy mixture was nearly dry, the powder was carefully applied. If the mixture were too wet, the bronze powder would sink into the varnish and lose its brilliance; but if it were in the proper tacky condition, the varnish would take just enough powder to give a bright, polished design. This free-hand bronze method, which was invented in 1812 by Thomas Hubbell of Clerkenwell, made an interesting contrast when combined with gold leaf.

Later, cathedral interiors were reproduced in bronze work known as the Wolverhampton style, for which the whole area was varnished. The tools were brushes, swabs, and paper templets, the latter being needed for a sharp straight or curved line. The templet was placed in position, and the powder carefully applied along the edge with a swab as in a simple form of stencilling. In the late nineteenth century cheaper stencilled tinware trays were introduced. It would be very unusual to find a papier-mâché tray that was entirely stencilled.

Shadows were made by using less and less powder, letting it disappear gradually into the black ground. Highlights and details were emphasized by using a swab made by twisting a piece of chamois into a shaft of a goose quill. This small swab was then dipped into a fine pale gold powder and used in the manner of a crayon or pencil. The worker had to work rapidly in order to complete the design before the varnish dried completely. Ecclesiastical figures were added with paint. These bronze interiors were known as the Wolverhampton style, because they were developed by

Frederick Perks in 1844, when he was employed at Ryton and Walton's. Bronze work can be found on Sandwich-edge trays, pole screens, letter racks, and hand screens.

After the death of Prince Albert in 1861, gray and mauve paint with mother of pearl was used, and articles painted in those subdued tones were called "ceremonial ware," though since that day the significance of this treatment has been overlooked or forgot.

Thousands of patterns were used, and, according to Henry Loveridge, each manufacturer had about two thousand. It is difficult to attribute any work definitely to individuals or to companies unless the article is signed. Popular ideas were often copied, and blank-makers turned out the same or similar shapes for all firms. Borders were transferred by one man, the pearl work was perhaps done by another, and the center was painted by an artist. Usually the designs were drawn onto paper and then carefully pin-pricked so evenly and beautifully that not a stray pinhole deviated from the outline. The pricked drawing was placed into position, and powder was pressed through the holes to leave an outline on the japanned surface over which the painter could work the design. In the Sheldon collection, now on display at The City Museum and Art Gallery in Birmingham, there are several numbered drawings of designs with color and pearl notes added, and on a few the names of workers, including a few pricked designs. There is also a collection of pattern books at the gallery in Wolverhampton, some of which belonged to the Loveridge company.

With very few exceptions, japanned wares were finished with a stripe or a line that followed the edges or other outline of the form, a practice carried over from the vehicle-japanners. Coaches, carriages, and later bicycles and early automobiles were picked out in fine lines on the body and the wheels, a work that required one special brush and a steady hand. A filleter, as he was called, or a liner or striper, was a specialist in the japanning trade. In 1845 George Sadler was a filleter at Frederick Walton's; he later moved to Loveridge's. After so many years at his specialty, Sadler was able to take a thirty-inch tray in his left hand, and with one sweep of the striping brush in his right hand he was able to draw a line around the edge of a tray. The outer edge of a tray provides a steadier guide, because the ring finger is kept under the edge as the thumb and first finger pull the

Figure 100: Tea board in the Clay style. The rim is bordered in two shades of bronze powders. A narrow gold-leaf Hepplewhite vine follows the edge of the tray floor. The oval painting in the center was added sometime later. *Figure 101:* An exceptionally fine example of early bronze-work ornament combined with gold leaf. The piece is a small tray in the Clay style.

loaded striping brush around the rim. When striping the floor of a tray, which is harder to do, the tip of the ring finger is lightly placed onto the floor of the tray, where it steadies and braces the hand as it follows along while the line is being made.

Rectangular and Gothic trays marked Loveridge, Walton & Co., or Clay have an unusual kind of stripe on the flat edge of the upturned rim. This edge is nearly three eighths of an inch wide and is covered with a gold stripe on which are superimposed black Chinese characters (*Figure* 77). In *Figure 78* the Clay tray shows an unusual small floral pattern on the flat edge. The same painter may have worked for all three houses, either painting in his own studio or perhaps changing jobs.

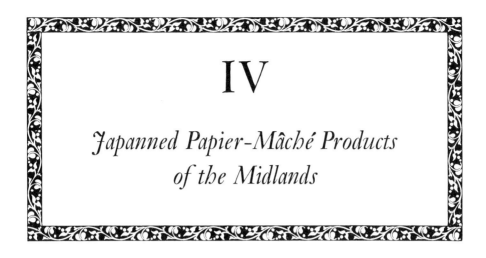

IV

Japanned Papier-Mâché Products
of the Midlands

Among the many inventions of modern times for diffusing the luxuries, and even the conveniences of life, there are few which have greater claims to our admiration than papier mâché. Whether it meets the eye in the shape of furniture, or in articles of domestic utility, its beauty and agreeableness are equally striking and effective. Nor is it less so when applied to ornamental purposes.
—The World in Its Workshops, by James Ward, 1851.

In the "black country" many bright and glittery articles were produced for the domestic and foreign markets. Brasses, cut steel buckles and other "toys," mother-of-pearl articles, pinchbeck jewelry, all kinds of buttons, and a bewildering variety of japanned metal and papier-mâché products. Most of the Birmingham products have at some time been scornfully called imitation, sham, cheap, or "Brummagem," but many of them still survive to be much sought after by collectors. One wonders if today's plastics, synthetic fabrics, and false jewelry are so different in quality, and if they will last for so long a time. Certainly there is nothing manufactured today that can show the elaborate handiwork on the japanned products of the Midlands, which because of labor costs, if for no other reason, would be an impossibility.

Quantities of Birmingham papier-mâché products have survived for our interest and pleasure. Many of the articles that were considered necessary or useful during the eighteenth and the nineteenth centuries are now

135

only curiosities, but they are admired for their beautiful or unusual ornamentation and as reminders of times past. Gone is the need for a hand screen, a card case, a spill vase (*Figure 103*), or snuffbox, although some pieces can be adapted for modern use: a snuffbox makes a pillbox, or a spill vase becomes a pencil-holder.

Small boxes were the earliest and the most popular product before the introduction of the tea tray. Whether of English or of European origin, signed or not, they are hard to resist. In the eighteenth century they were probably made in larger numbers than any other article of papier mâché until the end of the Georgian era, and the great demand for them kept the cost low. Not only were small boxes made for snuff, but for patches, the sugar-coated fruit, root, or seed called comfits, wafers, or bonbons. The boxes varied in size from tiny ones for ladies to those large enough to hold a supply of snuff for guests at inns or for family use or to hold a gentleman's tobacco (*Figures 107–109*).

It was important to handle a snuffbox correctly, as important as the handling of a fan or a card case. The box should, of course, have a hinged lid, and the snuff-taker, three hands, if he should attempt to follow the instructions offered by Charles Lillis and Company in *The Spectator* in August of 1711: "The exercise of the Snuff Box according to the most fashionable Airs and Notions in opposition to the exercise of the Fan will be taught with the best Plain and Perfumed Snuff." The correct technique was to remove the box from the pocket with the left hand, tapping the lid with the finger of the right hand three times before opening it. Then a pinch of snuff was removed, and the lid closed. The snuff was then placed on the back of the left hand or on the thumb nail enclosed by the forefinger, and finally inhaled.

The lids of the japanned boxes were ornamented with metal leaf, bronze powders, imitation tortoise shell, mother of pearl, and paint. Some bore landscapes, allegorical or romantic scenes, portraits of royal personages or other famous people, the majority taken from popular engravings. Many of the paintings were full of detail, especially Hogarth's *Midnight Modern Conversation* (*Figure 110*) and Tenier's *The Blind Fiddler*. To reduce such a painting by eye would not be practical if it were to be used often, so an outline drawing of the picture was made in the proper size and

Figure 102: Thirty-two-inch tea board in the Clay style, with the gallery nailed to the floor. The tray is ornamented with the conventional pineapples, which were considered a symbol of hospitality and so eminently suitable for a tray. These were done in bronze and gold leaf. *Figure 103:* A match-holder, on the right, and a spill-holder made in Wolverhampton sometime during the 1880s or 1890s, showing the influence of Japanese decorative arts of the second half of the nineteenth century.

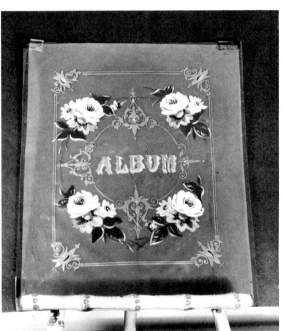

Figure 104: Die-pressed papier-mâché painted bowl without pearl. *Figure 105:* Small daguerreotype case with sides of papier mâché. *Figure 106:* Album with papier-mâché painted front showing a late Victorian design. *Figure 107:* Snuff box with colored engraving.

then traced onto the lid of the box. The colors were painted over this outline.

Early in the nineteenth century, small round prints or engravings on paper were made for the trade. These were glued to the box lids, hand-colored, and then varnished. These engravings were of views, portraits, and comic figures and of scenes from American life, all apparently made by James Smillie, a Scottish engraver who went to Quebec in 1823, by a man named Leney who emigrated from London to the United States in 1805, and by Samuel Maverick and Thomas Clark.

Although there were many japanner-painters employed in the Birmingham shops who decorated a large number of boxes in a day, their work is largely unidentified. Samuel Raven, who worked for himself, signed many of his boxes. Raven, who should not be confused with John Samuel Raven (1829–1877), a landscape-painter, was born in 1775 and died in 1847. Nothing is known of his early life as a painter, but it is thought that he worked for Small and Son, Guest, Chopping and Bill and left in 1816, when this company closed, to establish his own studio. He obtained the blank boxes from Small and Son, Guest, Chopping and Bill or their successor Jennens & Bettridge.

The snuffboxes and tobacco boxes painted by this skillful artist and sold from his studio in 1826 were inscribed in red letters inside the cover "S. Raven, Pinxt." Sometimes the title of the picture was added in white script so small that it is hard to see without a magnifying glass.

A young man known now only by his initials H. H. H. H., who was apprenticed to Raven from 1820 until 1827, said of him that he was a "man of talent but without much original power; all the boxes and cigar cases painted whilst I remained with him were copies. He purchased many engravings which he considered suitable for the purpose." The former apprentice also said that "Mr. Raven behaved well to me and I was permitted to commence the painting to which Raven added the finishing touches. These boxes were not signed." Samuel Raven was proud to write inside the lids of the signed boxes between 1815 and 1831: "Patronized by the Duke of Sussex and Prince Leopold of Saxe-Coburg" (*Figure 112*).

Morland was out of fashion during the 1820s, but game and figure pictures after Moses Haughton were used. Some of the subjects favored

Figure 108: Early English snuff box. *Figure 109:* English tobacco box, the picture on which was painted over a single piece of white pearl shell with transparent paint.

Figure 110: English snuff box depicting Hogarth's *Midnight Conversations*, by Samuel Raven. *Figure 111:* Snuff box decorated with a portrait of George IV by Samuel Raven, after the portrait of Sir Thomas Lawrence. *Figure 112:* Another snuff box with a painting of a terrier by Samuel Raven. *Figure 113:* The inside lid of the snuff box illustrated in *Figure 112* showing the usual signature of Samuel Raven in sealing-wax red paint.

Figure 114: Another snuff box painted by Samuel Raven, illustrating a miserly banker counting his money. *Figure 115:* English sewing box.

by Raven were *The Blind Fiddler, The Fair Penitent, Venus and the Doves, The Three Graces,* George IV (*Figure 80*), Mary, Queen of Scots, and Baskerville (*Figure 19*).

> For females fair and formal fops to please
> The mines are robbed of ore, of shells the seas
> With all that Mother Earth and beast afford
> To man unworthy now, tho' once their lord;
> Which wrought into a box, with all the show
> Of art the greatest artists can bestow,
> Charming in shape, with polish't rays of light,
> A joint so fine it shuns the sharpest sight,
> And precious stones that ere arrived in Thames.
> Within the lid the painter plays his part,
> And with his pencil proves his matchless art;
> There drawn to life some spark or mistress dwells,
> Like hermits chaste and constant in their cells.
>   —*Pandora's Box; A Satyr Against Snuff,* 1719.

Sewing boxes (*Figure 114*) were equipped with bodkins, punches, threadwinders, scissors, and thimble, some of these accessories in pearl or ivory. Then there were toilette or vanity boxes, and glove, fan, jewel and tea boxes as well as those made to hold checkers, cards, and chess pieces. For all these and for the larger caskets, the manufacturers needed silk, satin, patterned papers, or velvet linings, the sewing accessories, and the services of a tooler for edging the velvet and for preparing the leather bindings for folios and daguerreotype cases. For other articles, fancy metal furniture was required, such as white-metal and silver locks and keys, brass or bronze feet, handles and knobs, all Midlands products. Some tiny silver locks were stamped with a crown and the initials V. R. to indicate that the locksmith held a royal patent.

Related products of the paper-manufacturers were the dainty patterned papers for lining boxes and folios and an inexpensive substitute for jet. The long period of mourning by Queen Victoria after the death of the Prince Consort in 1861 created an unusual demand for jet among the ladies-in-waiting and others. Too, jet was much in vogue as an ornament for hats, dresses, and jewelry. A Birmingham paper-manufacturer devised a method

Figure 116: An example of the popular "ladies' companion," a box for the toilet table or for travelling. This one has an escutcheon of pearl and is painted and gilded on a dusted bronze ground. *Figure 117:* The inside of the "ladies' companion" illustrated in *Figure 116*, showing the crystal and silver fittings and the crushed red velvet lining of the lid.

Figure 118: Sewing and writing cabinet of wood covered in papier mâché and thoroughly decorated, *c.* 1845. *Figure 119:* The cabinet illustrated in *Figure 118* opened to display the interior.

145

Figure 120: Large tea board in the Clay style, illustrating the biblical story of Samuel and Eli, after the painting by John Singleton Copley, in the center of a gold-leaf frame. The border has leaves, shells, and strawberries done in gold leaf. *Figure 121:* A rare type of Windsor-edge rectangular tray, narrower in width than the standard type. The nacre still displays an exceptionally fine lustre, and this fact as well as the beautifully executed Oriental design indicate that it was an Oriental product.

of cutting and carefully japanning black paper to imitate jet, though by the end of the century the demand for this product had passed.

TRAYS

Tea reached England from Holland in the 1650s, and by the end of the seventeenth century the beverage had become so popular that the English East India Company shipped twenty thousand pounds annually, and the amount increased steadily beyond that. Tea became a national drink with the English, and it was important to have all the necessary apparatus for easily and correctly serving it. Tea tables, tea boards, and tea trays were introduced, and the Staffordshire potteries increased their production of cups and teapots that somewhat resembled Chinese porcelains. Then, among the majority of people, the vogue for anything Oriental became a mania, even though they saw no real distinction between the Chinese or the Japanese or either and the Indian.

It was tea then that was responsible for the introduction of the tray, and those finished in the imitation lacquer were made of sheet iron, tin-plate, leather-covered wood, and papier mâché. All were popular from the start.

The earliest paper tray was made from a rectangular panel with an attached upstanding rim or gallery, nearly two inches in height. The gallery was set into a groove in the edge of the panel and secured with nails and glue. Some Gothic trays were also put together in this way. In *Figure 123*, the nails are the tiny black dots seen on the broken rim. Oval gallery trays were a fairly early Clay product, and they are rare today. If this type were frequently carried by the handle holes cut in the gallery, the weight on the tray would eventually cause the floor and gallery to separate.

Another rectangular tray had a Sandwich edge or rim that was turned up about one half inch and then flattened horizontally. The flat portion varied in width from a narrow one half inch to an inch and a half. A Sandwich edge (*Figures 75 & 76*) was also used on Gothic trays as well as on the small, round, octofoil tray of either metal or papier mâché.

The Midlands manufacturers were always seeking new ideas for tray forms that would appeal to the general market. The Gothic shape, also called Chippendale, must have been well received, for it was introduced

Figure 122: Windsor tray *c.* 1850–1860, black with gilding, and inscribed Mapplebeck & Lowe.

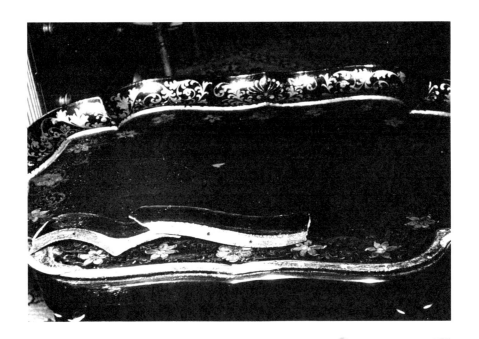

Figure 123: The broken rim of a Gothic tray. The small black dots on the underside are nails. *Figure 124:* King Gothic tray with a decorated stripe on the edge.

Figure 125: Oval trays with transfer borders made by the firm of Ebenezer Sheldon.

rather early in the nineteenth century and continued in popularity until the end of the industry. Although the name Chippendale was given to these trays, one can only guess that it was because the gadrooned edge was reminiscent of Chippendale furniture, not because the master cabinet-maker had anything to do with these trays. It is generally believed they were so named because they were considered a "true Chinese shape."

There were several variations of this form, but the most popular was the King Gothic (*Figures 73, 74 & 116*). The parlor-maid's tray or kidney-shaped tray (*Figure 72*) resembled the Gothic, but had an inward curve on one side that fitted the waistline and helped to support the weight of a heavily laden tray. At the time when Gothic trays were made on a die-press, a concave rectangular tray was also formed by the press. In 1855 these oval trays called Windsors were stamped out of metal and paper in great quantities and were especially advertised by several Wolverhampton firms. These cheaper trays with transfer borders and fewer coats of varnish were produced as a result of the development of the electroplating industry after 1840. There was a great demand for the new silverplated trays in place of the hand-painted papier-mâché trays, and this formidable competition caused a depression in the japanning industry. These trays are shown in company catalogues in various sizes with elaborate gold and white transfer-printed borders, each border having its own fanciful name (*Figures 56–59*).

In May of 1853 William S. Burton of Oxford Street in London advertised in some of the original monthly wrappers of Dickens's *Bleak House* as follows:

PAPIER MACHE AND IRON TRAYS

An assortment of TEA TRAYS AND WAITERS, wholly unprecedented, whether as to extent, variety and novelty.

Gothic shape Papier Mache Trays, per set of three . . . from 20 shillings to 10 guineas.

Convex shape, ditto . . . from 7 shillings.

A large quantity of small Papier Mache and Iron Trays, many of them executed in the highest style of art, at about a quarter of their original cost; being odd or slightly out of condition. These are especially worthy of the attention of Tavern and Coffee-house keepers. Round and Gothic Waiters, Cake and Bread Baskets, equally low.

By 1857 Burton had replaced the Gothic trays with the new oval papier-mâché trays, a set of three costing from twenty shillings to ten guineas. The new oval iron trays cost from four to thirteen guineas, a drop in price of two shillings and six pence in two years. These were probably the Wolverhampton products shown in their catalogues.

The large tea board illustrated in *Figure 133* was made of paper panel and measures thirty-two and three quarters inches in length. Its rim was formed over a mould and was then attached to the panel with small nails or glue. The handsome marine picture was painted by Robert Salmon in 1808; his initials and the year can be seen in the lower right corner of the picture.

According to the bulletin of The Worcester Art Museum (March, 1961), the years of Salmon's birth and death are not known, but his earliest dated pictures show that he was thoroughly competent in his art by 1800. It is known that he worked for a long time in Liverpool, and the shore line at the left of the picture recalls that of the Mersey River in Liverpool. It was from that port city that a large number of the Midlands japanned wares were shipped to the United States. Salmon was an accomplished marine painter, and it is doubtful that he was connected with the japanning industry. This particular tray was probably painted as a gift or on commission for someone with nautical interests, probably for Robert Ewell, the owner of the *Huntress*. Salmon, who was of Scottish background, later emigrated to Boston, where he worked with great success from 1828 until 1841.

The Salmon tea board is interesting for another reason as well. The picture was painted over some original ornament. Small chipped and worn spots on its wide border reveal bits of vermilion and gold leaf, and in the center of the tray a dark blue octagonal panel can be partially seen where the painting is worn. A stripe edged this panel and is still discernible near the edge of the painting. In the late nineteenth century an inexperienced japanner must have covered the original border with dark scrolls on a bronze ground. Through the years many trays and other similar articles were repainted or touched up, though few so interestingly as was this one. It is a good practice to inspect closely any piece, back and front, for one is often rewarded by the discovery of a mark or the name of a manufacturer or distributor.

Figure 126: Wine tray ornamented in pearl and ivory at Jennens & Bettridge, and designed by Richard Redgrave, A. R. A., for the Summerley Art Manufacturer of 1847. *Figure 127:* Early nineteenth-century wine coaster, painted and gilded with the feathering of the Prince of Wales on the side and peacock feathers on a black ground.

Figure 128: Wine coaster of red japan with free-hand bronze and etched gold-leaf ornament. *Figure 129:* Another wine coaster.

A wine tray was a Victorian product with a shallow well at each end in which to put a bottle or a decanter. Some of these were japanned at Jennens & Bettridge's, whose company perhaps made as well the handsome wine coasters with painted and gilt borders around the outside of the gallery illustrated in *Figures 126–129*.

Although octagonal trays made of sheet iron were plentiful, there were perhaps not so many made of papier mâché; at least, there are fewer in existence today. The tray in *Figure 80* is a fine example of free-hand bronze work and was probably made at the Old Hall Works, as is that in *Figure 102* with its gold leaf.

In addition to the larger trays there were the small salvers, card trays, snuffer trays, game-counter trays, and cake and bread baskets. Wolverhampton produced some interesting toy trays or doll's trays, but these were of metal.

Blank trays were a convenience for the japanner, and though the larger firms made their own blanks, there were several shops that specialized in this related industry. The price of blanks did not vary from early in the nineteenth century, but the discount allowed on purchases increased after fifty years until it reached ten per cent on all purchases of one hundred pounds. After the middle of the century a blank tray could be made with ready-made panel supplied by the paper mills and formed on a die-stamping machine, a faster and simpler process compared with the slow, laborious manual method. By 1870 the paper-sheet method had been abandoned entirely. James Neville, the brother of George, was a die-sinker, who made dies for the blank-makers and for Alsager & Neville. William Brindley, a tray-maker, also produced screw presses for the trade, and John Evans began making air pumps for paper-making machines about 1839.

LEATHER TRAYS

A rare type of tray that resembled papier mâché was made of thin japanned leather, glued to a wooden form. These trays were undoubtedly an offshoot of the eighteenth-century coachmakers industry and are an interesting development of tea boards from coach panels before the paper panels were used. The leather was japanned before it was applied to the wooden form, so that it was not necessary to stove the tray, which might

Figure 130: Handsomely decorated papier-mâché bioscope or stereoscope for viewing slides. *Figure 131:* Matching box for storing slides.

Figure 132: Superbly decorated tip-top table from Jennens & Bettridge, with their signature on the back. The beautifully colored painting, probably an adaptation of an oil original, depicts Jupiter's rape of Europa.

Figure 133: Large tea board, measuring 32 ¾ inches in length, with a handsome marine painting by Robert Salmon.

well have caused the wood to warp. These trays were made of well sea-soned deal with glue as a filler and an adhesive to hold the leather. The leather was coated with an elastic japan that could be folded without cracking the surface, a finish that was impervious to water "unless it be sea water which is very destructive." An example of the effect of sea water on a leather tray can be seen in *Figure 136*, one that was drenched during an Atlantic storm. An enemy of leather, especially for trays, was a cutting tool which may be one reason why there are so few in existence today.

BUTTONS

In the late eighteenth century the manufacture of japanned buttons became closely allied to the sheet-iron and papier-mâché trades. It is quite possible that papier-mâché buttons were introduced by Henry Clay, because in 1774 he obtained a patent for making them of paper panel, and later, in 1786, he patented a process for ornamenting them with pearl shell. Five years later he acquired yet a third patent, this one for making slate or stone buttons, which may have been japanned and decorated in similar fashion. Another maker of papier-mâché buttons was Obadiah Westwood, who may have worked for Clay at that time.

In the nineteenth century the discs were stamped out of button boards, which were strips of panel made in the required widths especially for the trade by paper-manufacturers. William Sheldon of Birmingham was making papier-mâché buttons and other wares in this manner in 1843. In 1851 James Souter and James Warton, also of Birmingham, devised a method by which a fly press, in one operation, stamped out the discs, drilled the holes, and formed a recess on the back of each disc to which a strengthening metal plate could later be added. The japanned papier-mâché buttons were then ornamented with gilt and pearl shell or with fluid glass, which was pressed through the button holes from underneath and looked like a projecting jewel. Some of later make were encased in metal rims; these are now rather rare.

Figure 134: Indian work on a papier-mâché bread basket without embossing.
Figure 135: Small tray with a painted rural scene.

Figure 136: Eighteenth-century leather tray, originally without the center painting. The painting is signed P. Spalding and is dated 1819. It was washed by sea water during a storm when it was stored in the hold of a transatlantic liner, hence the severe cracking. *Figure 137:* The floor of an oval eighteenth-century gallery tray in brown leather, with fine, restrained gold-leaf work in the Hepplewhite style.

HAND AND POLE SCREENS

Hand screens came in pairs, which suggest a twosome in conversation before the hearth. The heat-proof, rigid material 'intended becomingly to shade the face from the heat of the fire' was mounted onto a slender handle of turned or carved ebony, ivory, or gilded wood. The handles were at first riveted to the screen, but later were attached with a screw and a wing nut, permitting the handle to be tightened when necessary (*Figure 139*).

Hand or face screens were made of panel cut out with a bow-saw in roughly round, oval, or galeate shape, and had scrolled, voluted, scalloped, or dragooned edges.

All the familiar forms of ornamentation were used on the screens, and these attractive articles must have been conversation pieces when held in the hand or when placed on the mantelpiece. Although they are no longer a necessary item, the majority are fine examples of the japanner's art and are admired by collectors.

A pole screen was mounted on a wooden pedestal, which may have rested on a tripod or a papier-mâché base, and which could be adjusted to any desired height. A table screen was a small version of a pole screen to be placed on a table to shield the eyes from a candle or lamp flame (*Figure 142*).

PORTABLE OR LAP DESKS

A lap desk was a box with a slanted lid (*Figure 143*). Under the lid was a tooled, velvet-covered writing board that lifted up to reveal a space underneath for stationery. In front of the board was a slot for pens, a crystal bottle for ink, and a covered square box for sealing wafers. Each desk was fitted with a small white-metal or silver lock and key, and they were ornamented with gold, paint, and pearl shell, with the important work on the lid.

Thomas Lane of Birmingham and London patented the use of pearl glass panels set into the lid of the "Escritoires," as he called them, but not many of these can be seen in this country, perhaps because of the hazards of shipping them. The idea of combining glass panels with papier-mâché

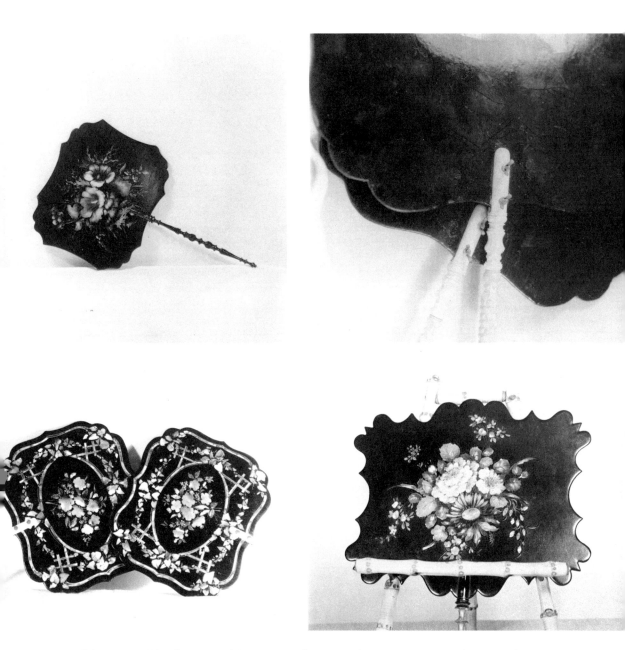

Figure 138: Hand screen with a teak or ebony handle. *Figure 139:* A close-up of
the piece illustrated in *Figure 138,* showing the wing-nut tighteners. *Figure
140:* Hand screens decorated with rainbow-colored mother of pearl and fitted
with carved ivory handles. *Figure 141:* Hand screen decorated with well executed flowers in pearl and paint on a black japanned ground.

Figure 142: Table screen made sometime about the end of the nineteenth century.

Figure 143: Portable desk by Ebenezer Sheldon. *Figure 144:* Papier-mâché ink stand fitted with a crystal bottle, a mother-of-pearl paper-knife and pen, and an agate pen. The papier mâché is ornamented in burnished and dull metal leaf.

Figure 145: Desk folio of 1864. *Figure 146:* Portable desk opened to display the velvet lining. *Figures 147, 148, 149:* Portable desks. *Figure 150:* Small patterned paper-lined desk folio of 1864.

Figure 151: Blotter, painted, with pearl decoration. *Figure 152:* Blotter, *c.* 1855–1860, on the front of which is painted a floral design, and on the back of which is a colored engraving of a country church. *Figure 153:* Blotter from the firm of Ebenezer Sheldon, showing the mania for "Japanism" prevalent in the 1880s. Note the asymmetrical arrangement somewhat in the Japanese style. *Figure 154:* Inkstand from McCallum & Hodson, decorated by Reuben Thomas Neale. The central section once held a box for sealing wafers.

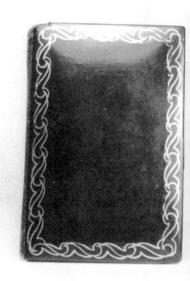

Figure 155: Folio-type card case by Jennens & Bettridge. *Figure 156:* Back of a card case by Jennens & Bettridge, *c.* 1816–1864. *Figure 157:* Card case made during the second half of the nineteenth century, with a Wolverhampton design also widely used on daguerreotype cases. *Figure 158:* Hinge-type card case, decorated in the Persian style, which was very popular for several years.

desks and other household 'elegancies' was suggested by Miss Eliza Tonge of Boston in Lincolnshire.

Other items manufactured for the business of letter-writing were desk envelopes, blotters, portfolios, albums, letter racks, and inkstands.

Inkstands were roughly oval or rectangular and stood on four flattened ball-feet of japanned wood. Like the lap desks, they had a slot for pens, a wafer box, and two cavities lined with velvet in which the ink bottles stood. Agate or mother-of-pearl pen-holders and paper-cutters were a product of the period and often accompanied the inkstand on a lady's desk.

CALLING-CARD CASES

Calling-card cases of papier mâché were made as early as 1826 and were carried by gentlemen and ladies throughout the Victorian era. The embossed calling cards were kept clean and smooth in the hinged cases lined in plush, silk, or paper. The silk linings were usually of red or deep rose. Those cases made for ladies' use were a little larger than those for gentlemen, whose pockets must not be made to bulge more than was absolutely necessary.

Just as with the snuffboxes and fans, there was a recommended procedure for correctly using the card case. Ladies were instructed to hold them in plain view while opening them to extract a card. It was also suggested that a fancy handkerchief be carried as an appropriate backdrop to the case!

CARD TRAYS

A card tray on the hall table was a necessary repository for calling cards. If one did not have a silver tray, the next best was an attractively gilded and painted papier-mâché card tray. They came with or without gilded bronze handles, and they were decorated with small versions of those designs popular on tea trays—flowers, birds, urns, fountains, and exotic birds, finished or framed with a lacy gold border.

Figure 159: Late nineteenth-century photograph album from the firm of Ebenezer Sheldon. *Figure 160:* Late nineteenth-century book slides by Ebenezer Sheldon.

Figure 161: The front of a blotter, *c.* 1870, decorated with a painting of the Vale of Berkley in Gloucestershire from an original oil painting. The decoration is a colored stippled engraving on papier mâché. The back is stamped with the royal arms and the name T. F. Griffiths and Company, patentees. *Figure 162:* Book bound with papier-mâché sides, 1856. The title is *Moss Rose.* The decoration was done with broken pearl in the cornucopia and paint. *Figure 163:* Papier-mâché candle-extinguisher with a gilded knob.

171

Figure 164: Card box decorated in the style called "ceremonial ware," which was popular after the death of the Prince Consort. The inlaid pearl is decorated with purple-grey and white varnishes. *Figure 165:* Top of a box, decorated with a hunting scene. *Figure 166:* Elaborately decorated board game with twelve counters and a matching box made for Edward VII, when he was Prince of Wales. The background is of black japan with gold Gothic foliage.

Figure 167: Upright work-cabinet from the firm of Ebenezer Sheldon. *Figure 168:* Small paneled screen, decorated with large leaves of scrap pearl shell dotted with bright gold, by Ebenezer Sheldon.

Figure 169: Vase of papier mâché on a tray of papier mâché. *Figure 170:* Handsomely decorated Victorian picture frame of papier mâché. *Figure 171:* Slightly damaged tabletop of thick papier mâché, decorated with a printed design and a few touches of gold-leaf brushwork added to the corners, late nineteenth century or early twentieth century.

Figure 172: Top for a tip-top table decorated with a broken pearl border show-ing Windsor castle.

FURNITURE

Papier-mâché furniture with certain portions made of wood was produced by Henry Clay early in the nineteenth century. For example, Queen Charlotte's console tables, mentioned earlier, undoubtedly had a top of handsomely painted paper panel, but the apron and support were probably of carved, gessoed, and gilded wood in the fashion of the period.

Many other manufacturers who followed Clay also made paper furniture, but it was Jennens & Bettridge who spent a number of years designing and testing furniture made entirely of papier mâché. In some things they were successful, but it was found that if the material were combined with wood or iron, the piece had a better chance of survival. It was also discovered that a piano case made entirely of paper panel proved to have no resonance, and wood had to be used for the case.

Few commercial advantages were overlooked by the often mentioned firm of Jennens & Bettridge. By mutual arrangement with Peyton and Harlow in connection with the furniture display at the Crystal Palace, the latter firm exhibited "Patent improved metallic bedsteads japanned to correspond with papier-mâché furniture exhibited by Jennens and Bettridge."

Many of the earlier tables had bases, pedestals, or legs of wood, but later in the century the moulded table tops had a bulbous, fluted, hollow pedestal through which was put a sturdy rod to hold the top firmly to the base. This, however, proved in time to be a weak spot and a difficult one to repair.

Cabinets, bookcases, a six-piece bedroom suite, and many other ambitious pieces were produced during the second half of the century. Although they may have been made partly of paper panel, paper-covered wood or iron, or entirely of wood, they are usually miscalled papier mâché because of the decoration.

For a time these Victorian elegancies went out of favor, but now good pieces are sought after by new generations. Unfortunately, many of the large and lovely pieces of japanned furniture that resided in cool English houses suffer in the overheated American houses causing them to warp, come apart, or, if gessoed, to crack. It is advisable to place furniture of this type in a room that can be kept at sixty-five to seventy degrees Fahrenheit.

Figure 173: Work-table of wood and papier mâché from the firm of Ebenezer Sheldon.

Figure 174: Elaborately decorated game table of japanned wood.

178

Figure 175: Chair of wood and papier mâché, *c.* 1850. *Figure 176:* Upholstered papier-mâché chair made by McCallum & Hodson for the Great Exhibition of 1851. *Figure 177:* Chair made of moulded paper panel, japanned, painted, and pearled. *Figure 178:* Mid-Victorian chair of wood and papier mâché decorated with a painting of Warwick Castle.

Figure 179: Large settee of wood and papier mâché, japanned and ornamented with pearl and paint.

A Listing of Other Papier-Mâché Wares

snuffboxes
comfit boxes
toilette boxes
sewing boxes
buttons
fans
glove boxes
knitting needles
tobacco boxes
jewel boxes
handkerchief boxes
tea boxes
teapoys
lap desks (escritoires)
blotting books
folios
letter racks
book and album covers
paper weights
stationery case
ink stands
easels
console tables
loo tables
tea tables
worktables
canterburys
caskets
cabinets
sconces
doorplates
tea trays, singly and in sets
game-counter trays
card trays
snuffers
wine trays and wine coasters
panels

tazzas
potpourri jars
shallow bowls
bread baskets
cake baskets
face screens
pole screens
folding screens
calling-card cases
daguerreotype cases
key racks
base of letter scales
base for casters
wall brackets
door knobs
hanging shelves
barometer cases
clock cases
game boards
furniture
panels for ship's cabins
panels for coaches
panels for furniture
spectacle cases
candle-extinguishers
bellows
vases
spill vases
match holders
mirror mounts
picture frames and pictures
napkin rings
comb-and-brush holder
crumbers
book slides
bioscopes

Figure 180: Elaborate suite of furniture made of wood and decorated papier mâché for the Great Exhibition of 1851. The matching floral panels were decorated with mother of pearl and remain in brilliant condition. The entire suite of furniture was priced at £1000 in 1958.

I

On Maintenance and Repair

THINK of your papier mâché as a valuable oil painting. Unless you were trained to do the work, you would not think of cleaning and repairing it, or you should not. Often a bad matter is made worse when a well-meaning person attempts "to restore" or "to brighten" a piece of papier mâché. So a word to the wise is sufficient: it is better *to leave it alone* or else to give it to a professional finisher.

To clean it, dust the article first with a soft cloth that has no loose thread that might catch in a piece of pearl shell or a chipped spot in the papier mâché. If the article is quite soiled, use a damp cloth and Ivory soap, and wipe the surface gently, drying it thoroughly afterwards. Do the front, back, sides, and bottom, not only to clean, but to prevent warping. When the article is dry, a light application of oil will brighten the surface. Lemon oil or any good, light furniture oil will do, sparingly applied to all sides. Often the paper has become so dry that it drinks in the moisture, and if the entire surface of the piece is rubbed, there will be less chance of warping. This is especially true of trays; the backs should be done as well as the front. Then, to be sure, lay the tray with its face down, and weight it lightly, leaving it for a few days.

If a tray has white spots or rings from moisture or alcohol, try rubbing the spots with oil. Some people advocate using a walnut meat or camphor oil. If the spots are old ones, more drastic treatment is necessary, but again the word is *caution*. It is the varnish that has turned white, but it is the varnish that protects the ornament on japanned wares. Denatured alcohol will remove the white spots, but it will also remove the varnish, without which the ornament is unprotected and can disappear too. With a soft cloth, quickly, lightly rub the spots, and when the spot has disappeared, stop! After the alcohol has evaporated and the surface is dry, the tray can be lightly oiled.

If you want to protect the surface from further wear, a coat of varnish may be applied. If you have never varnished anything, it would be best to give it to a professional finisher—I repeat—leave it alone. Avoid using shellac or spray varnish; use an all-proof spar varnish and a soft varnish brush or a nylon stocking rolled up inside itself to form a soft ball. Use the varnish sparingly in an atmosphere as free of dust as possible. Varnish front and back of the tray, and when it is dry, lay it with its face down and weight it to prevent warping.

Chipped or broken papier mâché can be repaired so that the spot cannot be found. Take a little of whiting, plaster of Paris, or patching plaster, an equal amount of thick black paint from the bottom of a can, and enough varnish to make a doughy mixture. The varnish binds the mixture and prevents its crumbling. It is seldom necessary to mix much, for if the break is large, it must be built up a little at a time. A teaspoonful of mixture is sufficient for a surface chip, which can be filled and then smoothed with a palette knife. When it is dry, smooth it with a fine sandpaper until it is level with the surface. If a small hole appears, add more mixture, sand it, and coat with varnish.

To build up a broken corner, place a piece of masking tape on the under side. This provides a wall against which to put the mixture and also keeps the under side flat while you work from the top. Smooth and shape the mixture with a palette knife and fingers, watching it as it dries, to be sure that it holds its shape. Leave the tape on the back until the patch is dry, then remove it, and with a fine emery-paper smooth the edges and the top and bottom. Coat the repaired spot with varnish, and if the first coat sinks in when it is dry, add another. Wood putty is readily available and can be used instead of the mixture, but I have had better results with the latter.

A large bite out of the edge of a tray requires a stanchion or framework to support the plaster mixture. With fine wire, or straight pins, if they are long enough, make a fence by pushing the ends of the wire into the paper layers at the side of the break. Then place wide masking tape along the underside and start to fill the area, adding more and more of the mixture until you reach the top edge. It need not be done all at once, but do all that you can while shaping and modelling it to match the edge of the article. When it is dry, sand it smooth. Fill any small cracks or holes left until the patch is satisfactorily shaped and dry and then coat it with varnish.

Missing pearl shell can be replaced by using the directions given on page 112.

Hinges on lids of boxes and desks have a V-shaped metal piece that fits into a socket. These come loose from constant wear, but they can be reset by using *Epoxee*. If the papier mâché has broken away from the back of the hinge, it can be patched with the mixture described above or with plastic wood, then painted and varnished.

These V-shaped metal parts often break off the hinge. Craftsmen are afraid to solder on a new piece for fear of scorching the finish on the papier mâché. This was a problem that occurred with the fine desk shown in *Figure 000*.

Finally, I took two glazier's points, put them together with metal *Epoxee*, and attached them to the hinge with the same medium. After the proper drying time had elapsed, I reset the lid and patched the broken papier mâché at the socket. How permanent the repair will be remains to be seen as this was a recent experiment, but so far all is well.

If you have read this book, you will have learned that the work of ornamenting papier mâché was varied and specialized and took time to learn to perform it properly. It would be better to avoid patching worn gold spots with gold paint or even with gold, because it is impossible to match the gold, and even when the spot is dulled by what is generally termed "antiquing," it is still noticeable. Antique wares, though worn, are more valuable than any that are repainted or touched up, and it is much better to have a worn spot on a piece otherwise whole and sturdy.

II
Glossary

ASPHALT OR ASPHALTUM

A smooth, hard, brittle black or brownish-black resinous bituminous mineral consisting of a number of hydrocarbons and found in many parts of the world; called pitch, Jewish pitch, and, in the Old Testament, "slime."

COLECYNTH OR COLEQUINTIDA

An herbaceous vine indigenous to Africa and the other Mediterranean countries and related to the watermelon, from which a powerful cathartic is prepared; called bitter herb, bitter cucumber, and bitter gourd.

DRAGON'S BLOOD OR CINNABORIS

The bright red gum or resinous exudation on the fruit of the palm, a tree bearing a fruit not unlike the cherry.

DUTCH METAL

An alloy of zinc and copper beaten into leaves for use as a substitute for gold leaf; sometimes called Dutch foil or Dutch gold.

FACTOR

An agent or broker, a "doer" as the name implies; usually a representative of principals.

FILLETING

Ornamenters' term for the process of lining, striping, or picking out the design on a japanned article.

GUM ARABIC

An exudation of various species of acacia growing chiefly in the Sudan.

IMPASTO

The thick application of pigment on a painting or other work by using a mixture of gesso and glue or varnish.

ISINGLASS

A firm, whitish transparent glue made from the bladders of sturgeon and other fish.

PENCIL

The old term for a small brush of bristle or other hair, usually for fine work.

PINCHBECK

An alloy of copper and zinc invented by and named for Christopher Pinchbeck, a watchmaker, in 1732; often used for cheap jewelry during the eighteenth and nineteenth centuries.

PONTYPOOL

A town in Monmouthshire where articles of sheet iron and tinplate were made and japanned; finally a generic term for Midlands-made japanned tinware.

TAZZA

A shallow ornamental bowl or vase on a pedestal, sometimes having handles.

TOLE

The French word for sheet iron or painted tin.

TRAGACANTH

A mucilaginous substance derived from various low spiny shrubs of the genus Astragalus.

List of References

Books

Allen, George C. *The Industrial Development of Birmingham and the Black Country, 1860–1927*. London: Allen & Unwin, 1929.

Andès, Louis E. *Die Fabrikation der Papiermaché- und Papierstoff-Waren*. Vienna and Leipzig: A. Hartleben, 1922.

Bakushinsky, A. V. *Iskusstvo Mstery*. Moscow and Leningrad: 1934.

Barber, Edmund. *Painters', Grainers' and Writers' Assistant*. London: H. Elliot, 1852.

Bielefeld, Charles F. *On the Use of the Improved Papier-mâché in Furniture, in the Interior Decoration of Buildings, and in Works of Art*. London: 1850.

Birmingham and Midland Institute, Archaeological Section. *Transactions*. Vol. XXX, 1904.

Boswell, James. *The Life of Johnson*. Boston: Little, Brown, 1847.

Great Britain. East India Company. *The Register of Letters . . . of the Company . . . , 1600–1619*. Edited by Sir G. Birdwood. London: B. Quaritch, 1893.

Brooks, Jerome. *Tobacco; Its History Illustrated by the Books, Manuscripts, and Engravings in the Library of George Arents, Jr*. New York City: The Rosenbach Company, 1937–1952.

Restif de la Bretonne. *Les Nuits de Paris*. New York City: Random House, 1964.

Burton, Elizabeth. *The Pageant of Elizabethan England*. New York: Scribner, 1959.

Cennino, Cennini. *Il Libro Dell'Arte*. London: Oxford University Press, 1932–1933.

    Volume 1. Text, edited by Daniel V. Thompson.

    Volume 2. *The Craftsman's Handbook*, translated from the Italian by Daniel V. Thompson.

Chambers, Ephraim, compiler. *Cyclopaedia*. London: James and John Knapton, 1728. In two volumes.

Court, William H. B. *The Rise of the Midland Industries, 1600–1838*. London: Oxford University Press, 1938.

Curtis, Mattoon M. *The Story of Snuff and Snuff Boxes*. New York City: Liveright Publishing Co., 1935.

Dashwood, Charles J. "Pearl-shelling Industry in Port Darwin and Northern Territory," from *The Records of the Proceedings and the Printed Papers in the Sessions of the Parliament of the Commonwealth of Australia*, Session 1901–1902, Volume 2, 1902.

Davenant, Charles. *Discourses on the Publick Revenues, and on the Trade of England*. London: J. Knapton, 1698.

Davenport, Cyril J. H. *The Art Student's Vade-mecum*. London: Methuen, 1925.

Debo, Paul. *Aus der Geschichte einer Curieusen Kunst*. Wiesbaden: K. Albert, 1937.

Dent, Robert K. *The Making of Birmingham*. London: Simpkin, Marshall & Company, 1894.

Dent, Robert K. *Old and New Birmingham*. Birmingham: Houghton and Hammond, 1879.

Dickinson, George. *English Papier-mâché*. London: The Courier Press, 1925.

Dodd, George. *The Curiosities of Industry*. London: G. Routledge & Company, 1853.

Dossie, Robert. *The Handmaid to the Arts*. London: Printed for J. Nourse, 1st edition, 1758; 2nd edition, 1764.

Drake, James, publisher. *The Picture of Birmingham*. Birmingham: 1825.

Emerson, Edwin. *A History of the Nineteenth Century*. New York City: P. F. Collier and Son, 1902.

Fitzmaurice, Edmond G. *Life of William, Earl of Shelburne* (2nd edition). London: Macmillan, 1912.

Flexner, James T. *George Washington: The Forge of Experience, 1732–1775*. Boston: Little, Brown, 1965.

Gandee, B. F. *The Artist, or, Young Ladies Instructor in Ornamental Painting, Drawing, etc*. London: Chapman and Hall, 1835.

Gerard, Frances A. *Angelica Kauffmann*. London: Ward and Downey, 1892.

Gottesman, Rita S. *The Arts and Crafts in New York, 1726–1776* New York City: Printed for The New-York Historical Society, 1938.

Hart-Davis, Rupert. *Hugh Walpole*. New York City: Macmillan, 1952.

Hayward, Helena, editor. *The Connoisseur's Handbook of Antique Collecting*. London: *The Connoisseur*, 1960. A monograph.

Honour, Hugh. *Chinoiserie*. New York City: Dutton, 1962.

Houghton, John, editor. *A Collection for Improvement of Husbandry and Trade*. London: 1692–1703.

Hunter, Dard. *Chinese Ceremonial Paper*. Chillicothe, Ohio: The Mountain House Press, 1937.

Hunter, Dard. *Papermaking Through Eighteen Centuries*. New York City: W. E. Rudge, 1930.

Hutton, William. *An History of Birmingham* (4th edition). London: 1819.

John, William D. *Pontypool and Usk Japanned Wares*. Newport, England: The Ceramic Book Company, 1953.

Jones, W. H. *The Story of Japan and Tin Plate Working*. London: Alexander & Shepheards, 1900.

Ketton-Cremer, Robert W. *Horace Walpole*. Ithaca, New York: Cornell University Press, 1964.

Kingsbury, John. *Deadly Harvest*. New York City: Holt, Rinehart and Winston, 1965.

Koizumi, Gunji. *Lacquer Work*. London, New York City: Sir I. Pitman & Sons, Limited, 1923.

Latimer, John. *The Annals of Bristol in the Seventeenth Century*. Bristol, England: William George's Sons, 1900.

Lockyer, Charles. *An Account of the Trade in India*. London: Printed for the Author and sold by S. Crouch, 1711.

MacNamara, Desmond. *A New Art of Papier Mâché*. London: Arco Publications, 1963.

Mallett, Lady Marie. *Life With Queen Victoria*. Edited by Victor Mallett. Boston: Houghton, Mifflin, 1968.

Manners, Lady Victoria. *Angelica Kauffmann, R. A.* London: John Lane, 1924.

Molnár, Ferenc. *Angel Making Music*. New York City: Smith & Haas, 1935.

Montagu, Lady Mary Wortley. *The Complete Letters of Lady Mary Wortley Montagu*. Edited by Robert Halsband. Oxford: The Clarendon Press, 1965– .

Nesbitt, Alexander. *Lettering*. New York City: Prentice-Hall, 1950.

Orilia, Enrico. *La Madreperla e il Suo Uso Nell'industria a Nelle Arti*. Milan: U. Hoepli, 1908.

Palmerston, Henry T. *Portrait of a Golden Age; Intimate Papers*. Compiled and edited by Brian Connell. Boston: Houghton, Mifflin, 1958.

Penny, Virginia. *The Employments of Women: a Cyclopedia of Woman's Work*. Boston: Walker, Wise & Company, 1863.

Pepys, Samuel. *The Diary of Samuel Pepys*. Edited by Henry B. Wheatley. London and New York City: G. Bell & Sons, 1893–1899.

Perry, Josephine. *The Paper Industry*. New York City and Toronto: Longman's Green and Company, 1946.

Printer's, Gilder's and Varnisher's Manual. London: M. Taylor, 1830.

Prosser, Richard B. *Birmingham Inventors and Inventions*. Birmingham: Privately printed, 1881.

Ramsey, L. G. G., editor. *The Concise Encyclopedia of Antiques*. New York City: Hawthorn Books, 1955–1961. In five volumes.

Roe, Frederic G. *Victorian Furniture*. London: Phoenix House, 1952.

Simmonds, Peter L. *The Commercial Products of the Sea*. London: Griffith and Farran, 1879.

Simmonds, Peter L. *A Dictionary of Trade Products*. London: 1858.

Simmonds, Peter L. *Science and Commerce*. London: R. Hardwicke, 1872.

Smith, John T. *Nollekens and His Times*. London: [Henry Colburn,] 1828.

Stalker, John and George Parker. *A Treatise of Japanning and Varnishing*, Oxford: Printed and sold by the Author, 1688.

Stone, Leonard. *The Versatile Mr. Baskerville*. Chiswick, England: Chiswick Polytechnic School of Art, 1905.

Strange, Edward F. *Catalogue of Chinese Lacquer*. London: Victoria & Albert Museum, 1925.

Swinnerton, Frank A. *The Bookman's London*. Garden City, New York: Doubleday, 1952.

Thane, Elswyth. *Washington's Lady*. New York City: Dodd, Mead, 1960.

Timmins, Samuel. *A Collection of the Resources, Products and Industrial History of Birmingham*. London: R. Hardwicke, 1866.

Toller, Jane. *Papier-Mâché in Great Britain and America*. London: G. Bell & Sons, 1962.

Turberville, Arthur S. *Johnson's England*. Oxford: The Clarendon Press, 1933.

Turner, William. *Transfer Printing on Enamels, Porcelain and Pottery*. London: Chapman and Hall, 1907.

Yapp, George W. *Art Industry*. London: J. S. Virtue, 1879.

Periodicals

Annals of Science: Volumes 6, 7, 8; 1948–1952.

Antique Dealer and Collector's Guide: August, 1948.

Antiques: November, 1945; May, 1966.

Antiques Journal: February, 1962.

Apollo: May, 1956; December, 1962.

Art-Union Journal: 1847–1849.

Birmingham Magazine of Arts and Industries: Volume 1, Number 4; 1904.

Burlington Magazine: Volume 20; 1912.

Chamber's Journal: 1922.

The Connoisseur: January, 1929; June, 1929; August, 1931; August, 1967.

Country Life: Volume 1– ; 1897– ; very many relevant articles.

Decorator: Volume XII, Number 2; 1965.

Gentleman's Magazine: Volume VI; February, 1736.

Illustrated Exhibitor and Magazine of Art: 1852.

The Illustrated Midland News: Volumes 1–4; 1869–1870.

The Illustrated London News: Volume 1– ; 1842–

International Studio: Volumes 1–99; 1897–1931.

Just Buttons: March, 1947.

The London Tradesman: Volumes 1–5; 1808–1815; 2nd edition, 1820.

Magazine of Art: 1887.

Studio: Volume 92; 1926.

Universal Magazine: November, 1752.

Work: Volume 67; August, 1924.